AF589224

Healthyish HIGH PROTEIN

Emma Petersen

PAVILION

Contents

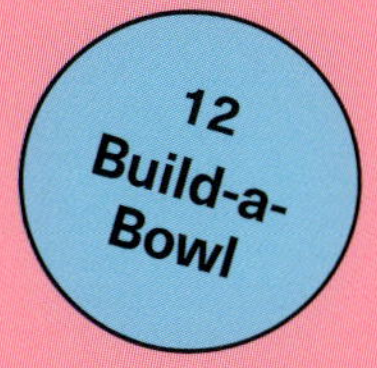

Welcome to Healthy-ish High Protein!

Writing a second cookbook still feels SO surreal, so first and foremost, thank you for making this possible.

When Healthy-ish came out last year, I hoped people might enjoy the recipes. I never quite expected the incredible response we had, and it meant so much. Not just because it was amazing to see so many of the recipes I developed over months appearing in your kitchens, but because of the messages of relief that came with them. Relief at finding a way of eating that was easy, delicious and didn't demand perfection. Relief at discovering that we are allowed to sit in the middle ground – to nourish our bodies and enjoy our lives at the same time.

That's Why This Book Exists.

A sequel, if you like. Because the world hasn't become any quieter. We're still surrounded by noise: what to cut out, what to track, what to fear. Somewhere along the way, even protein – something our bodies require on a daily basis – became wrapped up in marketing ploys, rules and extremes. It became a number to hit, a target to chase and another area where we're told we're either doing it 'right' or 'wrong'.

I don't believe in that.

The whole point of a *Healthy-ish* approach is to challenge diet culture's all-or-nothing thinking. Yes, we all want to eat well, but there is nothing healthy about a diet that leaves you miserable, under-fuelled or afraid of enjoying food. A sustainable way of eating has flexibility, ease and enough joy that means you want to keep going.

Healthy-ish High Protein is the next chapter of that story. And the clue is in the title.

The next thing I need to clear up is – no – this is absolutely not a gym-bro protein book. I am not here to teach you how to count your macros or get shredded (sorry). This is a real-life, flavour-first, joy-still-matters kind of book.

Like last time, this book follows the same Healthy-ish principles: real ingredients, minimal faff and an enormous respect for flavour. The difference here is simply a sharper focus on two very important nutrients: protein and fibre. Together they play a huge role in keeping us feeling full, focused and energized long after we've eaten. We could all benefit from eating more of them, we just don't need to lose our minds in the process. But more on that in a minute.

Another update since the last book: somewhere in between recipe testing and filming videos in my tiny London kitchen, movement became a bigger part of my life again. Running led to cycling, which led to swimming and, because I apparently enjoy pain, to training for a full-distance Ironman – which I completed in South Africa last month (April 2026). That experience – where food so obviously became fuel – was the best reminder that nutrition is so much more than hitting (often arbitrary) numbers. When we pay attention and notice what keeps us steady, energized and actually feeling good in our bodies, we learn far more than an app or a macro target could ever teach us. That lesson applies whether you're training for a 12-hour race (hi!) or simply getting through Tuesday. And protein and fibre sit right at the centre of that.

Inside this book you'll find easy breakfasts that actually tide you over till lunch, a huge variety of quick and easy dinners that don't take all night, fresh ideas for protein-packed lunches you can eat in or take on the go, and of course plenty of delicious sweet things, because joy is part of nourishment too.

So without further ado, here's to eating more protein and fibre – in the most delicious, Healthy-ish way.

Let's cook!
Emma x

Why do Protein + Fibre Matter?

Over the years, I've swung between obsessing over calories and macros to being so relaxed that nutrition barely crossed my mind. Unsurprisingly, one extreme wasn't great for my mental health, and the other wasn't great for my physical health. And neither helped me understand what actually made me feel good. As I mentioned, what finally shifted things was paying attention – not to numbers or rules, but to how I felt after eating.

I realised that the meals that kept me feeling energized and satisfied (i.e. not hunting down a snack 20 minutes later) had two things in common: protein and fibre.

Here's why.

PROTEIN
Protein is the builder

We've been sold the idea for so long that protein is only for 'fitness people'. That it's only really about building muscle, macros and hitting your targets. In reality, protein has far bigger jobs to do. Your body uses it constantly – to repair tissue, build hormones, produce enzymes and antibodies, and basically keep every cell functioning properly. It's working in the background all day long, whether you're lifting weights, lifting toddlers or lifting your laptop lid for the tenth time. Therefore, it deserves to be a focus for us all.

So... how much do we actually need?

The honest answer: it depends on things like your age, sex, activity levels and overall health. The UK's official minimum recommendation is around 0.75 g of protein per kilogram of body weight per day, but that amount is really just to keep the lights on at a cellular level. There are ways to work out a more personalized target that I sadly don't have space to dive into here (just make sure the calculators you use are designed by doctors, registered dietitians or NHS-type organizations). However, most experts encourage healthy adults to aim for 1–1.2 g per kilogram of body weight, which tends to support recovery, strength and everyday energy better than the bare minimum.

Does where it comes from matter?

Short answer: yes.

For a long time, 'high protein' to me meant bars, shakes and lean meat. I bought into the idea that if something had 20 g printed on the front, that made it a better choice. But the more obsessed I became with protein, the more processed my food became and the more restrictive my diet became, too – and that didn't make me feel good either. We've moved forward a little bit since then, thankfully, but there's still a way to go.

This book brings the focus back to where protein naturally lives: real food. Whole ingredients. Variety. A mix of both animal and plant-based sources.

Some protein sources, like meat, fish, eggs, dairy, soy and quinoa, are known as 'complete' proteins, meaning they contain all nine essential amino acids. Others, like beans, lentils, nuts, seeds and most grains, are known as 'incomplete', but that doesn't make them less valuable. It has long been proven that you don't need every amino acid in one meal; your body completes the puzzle across the day when you eat a variety of foods.

That's why variety sits at the heart of this book.

A high-protein diet does not need to mean turning every snack into a protein snack, or sneaking chicken into things that should not involve chicken. It's the bigger picture that counts – not perfection on one plate.

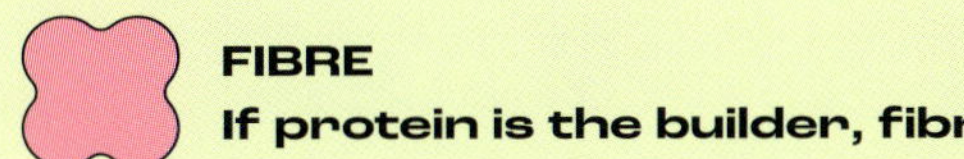

FIBRE

If protein is the builder, fibre is the balancer.

And thank goodness this underdog nutrient is finally having its moment. It doesn't shout about itself. Nobody stands in the yogurt aisle comparing grams of fibre on the label or announces, 'I'm going high-fibre this month.' But they should, because fibre quietly does a huge amount of good. It keeps digestion happy, supports your gut microbes (which has a knock-on effect on everything from energy to mood), and helps keep blood sugar and appetite steady, so you stay satisfied rather than hunting for something else to eat. And yet, most of us aren't getting anywhere close to enough. The UK average sits around 18 g a day, when the goal is closer to 30 g.

The good news is that you don't have to live on bran flakes to get there (although I do love them). Beans, lentils, oats, fruit, veggies, seeds and wholegrains all count. Basically, the more colour and plants on your plate, the better. What I found (without trying to be perfect about it) is that fibre shows up naturally when you're eating real food. So this book should make that deliciously easy for you, too.

THE BALANCE

When protein and fibre show up together (alongside healthy fats, micronutrients and all the other good things), food becomes genuinely satisfying. Protein keeps you full and supports your body; fibre keeps energy steady and digestion happy. That's the sweet spot this book lives in.

These recipes don't exist to help you hit a perfect number. You can trust that they're balanced and nourishing – I've done that work, so you don't have to. The goal here is simple: real food, a mix of protein and fibre, and enough flavour that you actually want to cook it again tomorrow.

That's sustainable healthy eating – and what *Healthy-ish High Protein* is all about.

How to Use This Book

Each recipe in this book is designed to make eating well simple and flexible. As this is a high protein book, you'll find the protein and fibre counts listed with every recipe. They're there for context, not control. As before, there are dietary swaps throughout, so most recipes can be adjusted to suit different preferences or needs.

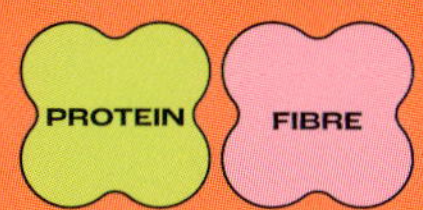

Each recipe comes with a protein and fibre count per serving.

DIETARY KEY AND SUBSTITUTIONS

- V **Vegetarian:** The recipe contains no meat or fish, but may include dairy and eggs.
- V/O **Vegetarian Option:** There are substitutions listed to make the recipe meat-free.
- VE **Vegan:** The recipe contains no animal products, including meat, dairy, eggs and honey.
- VE/O **Vegan Option:** Choose dairy-free milk, cheese, yogurt, cream, etc., and check the substitutions for other swaps to make the dish plant-based.
- DF **Dairy-Free:** The recipe contains no dairy products, like milk, butter or cheese.
- DF/O **Dairy-Free Option:** This recipe can be made dairy-free by choosing dairy-free milk, cheese, yogurt, cream, etc.
- GF **Gluten-Free:** The recipe is free of gluten, a protein found in wheat, barley and rye.
- GF/O **Gluten-Free Option:** There are substitutions listed to make the recipe gluten-free.
- N **Contains Nuts:** The recipe includes nuts.
- NF/O **Nut-Free Option:** There are substitutions listed to make the recipe nut-free.

Every recipe also has a Future You note, with guidance on storing leftovers, freezing portions or reheating – so you can cook once, and benefit twice.

The recipes are grouped by how we actually eat throughout the day, and this really is an everyday book. Mix and match across chapters, build meals that suit your schedule or just dip in when you need some midweek inspiration. There's no perfect way to eat Healthy-ish, only the way that feels good to you.

A NOTE ON LEFTOVERS

Although I've designed these recipes to minimize leftovers, sometimes you may find yourself with a bit of something extra – like a half-used pot of yogurt, for instance. Rather than letting it go to waste, flip to the index. There, you'll find all the other recipes that use that same ingredient, making it easy to incorporate into another dish later in the week. This will not only reduce food waste, but simplify meal planning, as you can build your meals around the ingredients you already have.

Eggs

Eggs are a source of 'complete' protein. Plus, they're quick to cook, endlessly adaptable and ideal for any meal of the day. Whether you like them just-set and jammy or scrambled and creamy, knowing how to nail your timings (and when to stop cooking!) will make all the difference. Here's how to get them right every time, plus some ideas for how to use each.

POACHED

Bring a pan of water to a gentle simmer and add a splash of vinegar. Crack an egg into a ramekin, then slide it into the water. Let it poach undisturbed for 3–4 minutes until the whites are set but the centre is still runny. Lift the egg out with a slotted spoon and drain briefly on kitchen paper/paper towels.

Serving suggestion:

Ideal for grain bowls, avocado toast or on top of stews for a hit of richness.

FRIED

Heat a drizzle of oil in a non-stick pan over medium heat and crack in an egg. Let it cook until the whites are set and the yolk is still soft. For crispy, lacy edges, use a touch more oil and allow the egg to sizzle. For over-easy, flip gently once the whites have set and cook for another 30 seconds or so.

Serving suggestion:

Provides an instant upgrade to rice bowls, curries, or added to leftovers for a protein boost.

SCRAMBLED

Crack 2–3 eggs into a jug or bowl with a splash of milk and pinch of salt. Whisk until smooth. Warm a drizzle of oil in a non-stick pan over low heat, then pour in the eggs. Stir gently, pushing them from the edges into the centre until they look just set and still glossy. Take the pan off the heat while they're slightly underdone – they'll continue cooking in the residual heat and stay soft and silky.

Serving suggestion:

Add cottage cheese for extra protein, or stir through herbs, feta and greens. Perfect in wraps, on toast, or as a quick lunch bowl base.

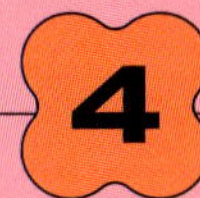

SOFT TO HARD-BOILED

Bring a pan of water to the boil (ensure it will fully cover the eggs), then lower the eggs in with a slotted spoon. Start the timer the moment they hit the water and follow the timings below. Cool the eggs immediately in cold water to stop them cooking further.

5–6 MINUTES	→	soft, runny centre
7–8 MINUTES	→	jammy yolk
9–10 MINUTES	→	firm but not chalky
11 MINUTES	→	hard-boiled

Serving suggestion:

Use in salads and bowls, mash for egg mayo or stash in the fridge (shell-on) for up to 5 days.

Build-a-Bowl

This is the formula I come back to again and again – the blueprint for building a bowl that's colourful, satisfying and properly balanced. Start with a hearty base, add a protein, layer in something fresh and crunchy and finish with a sauce that ties it all together. Mix and match depending on what you've got at home, or follow the cross-references to recipes throughout the book.

Choose one from each column ➜ combine in a bowl ➜ done.

BASE

Think fibre, texture and something to soak up the sauce.

- **Grains**: brown rice, quinoa, bulgur, couscous, soba noodles
- **Leafy:** kale, spinach, mixed leaves, cabbage slaw
- **Rooty:** roasted sweet potato, squash, white potato

In the book:

Burst Tomato Lentil Bowl (see page 120), Smoked Mackerel Potato Salad (see page 58)

PROTEIN

The anchor. This is what makes the bowl filling and keeps energy steady.

- **Meat and fish:** chicken, salmon, prawns/shrimp, canned fish
- **Plant-based:** tofu, tempeh
- **Dairy:** halloumi, cottage cheese
- **Other:** eggs, beans, lentils, edamame

In the book:

See... everything!

SAUCE

The magic element that brings everything together.

- **Vinaigrette** (Corn + Kale Pasta Salad, *see page 53*)
- **Sriracha dressing** (Sticky Tempeh Bowl, *see page 123*)
- **Creamy honey mustard** (Smoked Mackerel Potato Salad, *see page 58*)
- **Aji verde** (Mango, Avocado + Halloumi Salad With Aji Verde, *see page 56*)
- **Whipped tahini** (Chicken Skewers with Bulgur + Whipped Tahini, *see page 82*)
- **Sesame dressing** (Crispy Rice Salad, *see page 112*)
- **Pea-sto** (Broccoli Pea-sto Pasta, *see page 116*)
- **Tzatziki** (Herb-Crusted Salmon With Mustardy Potatoes, Tzatziki + Crispy Capers, *see page 87*)
- **Caesar** (Smashed Caesar Tacos, *see page 156*)
- **Hummus** (Harissa Tofu + Hummus, *see page 88*)

ADD ON

For crunch, freshness, colour and balance.

- Legumes: chickpeas/garbanzo beans, beans, lentils
- Quick-pickled onions
- Shredded cabbage or carrot
- Fresh herbs: coriander/cilantro, parsley, mint, basil
- Toasted nuts or seeds
- Avocado
- Tomato
- Cucumber
- Sweetcorn
- Kimchi
- Olives or capers
- Pickled jalapenos
- Jarred red (bell) peppers
- Pomegranate, mango or citrus segments

In the book:

Corn + Kale Pasta Salad (see page 53), Mango, Avo + Halloumi Salad (see page 56)

Tofu

Tofu is a protein powerhouse that takes on any flavour you give it. The key is knowing which type to use and how to prep it so it cooks up crisp and golden or creamy rather than bland. Whether you're frying, baking or scrambling it, this page breaks down the basics so you can turn one simple block into countless delicious meals.

PRESSING

This is the first step to better texture, but not always essential as many extra-firm tofus are already pressed, so always check the pack. If it feels dense and spongy straight from the box, you can skip this. Otherwise, drain the tofu, pat it dry, wrap it in a clean tea/dish towel and press under a weight for 10–15 minutes. This helps remove excess moisture, helping it crisp and soak up marinades. Note: silken tofu never needs pressing.

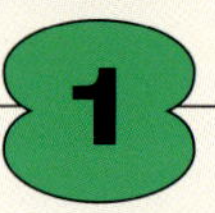

CUBED + FRIED

Cut extra-firm tofu into cubes and toss with cornflour, salt, pepper and a drizzle of oil. Fry in a non-stick pan over medium–high heat until crisp and golden on all sides. Add any sauce only at the end so the edges stay crunchy. Golden edges, chewy centre – ideal for bowls or curries.

In the book:

Tofu Thai Green Curry (see page 107) and Palak Tofu (see page 118).

TORN + BAKED

Tear extra-firm tofu into bite-sized chunks. Toss with cornflour, salt, pepper and a drizzle of oil. Bake at 200°C fan/220°C/425°F/gas mark 7 for 20 minutes, flipping halfway, until golden and crisp at the edges. More edges = more flavour. The inside stays soft, the outside goes crunchy, and it drinks up sauce afterwards.

In the book:

Gochujang Tofu Bowls (see page 115) and Burst Tomato Lentil Bowl (see page 120).

GRATED + BAKED

Use the coarse side of a box grater to grate extra-firm tofu straight into a bowl. Toss with cornflour, salt, pepper and a drizzle of oil. Spread onto a lined tray and bake for 15 minutes until crisp and browned. A shortcut 'tofu mince'.

In the book:

Loaded Fries (see page 94) and Harissa Tofu + Hummus (see page 88).

SCRAMBLED

Crumble firm and preferably smoked tofu into a hot pan with a drizzle of oil. Season with ground turmeric and garlic and add a splash of plant milk to loosen, then cook until heated through and lightly golden. Finish with nutritional yeast, pesto or lemon juice for richness. A savoury, protein-rich swap for scrambled eggs.

In the book:

Power Breakfast: Two Ways (see page 28).

SILKEN + BLENDED

Unlike firm tofu, silken tofu is usually sold shelf-stable (find it in the world food/ Asian food aisle). Drain, then add to a blender and blitz until smooth. Combine with a plethora of additional ingredients to make delicious sauces and dressings. For ultra-smooth sauces and dressings without cream.

In the book:

Silken Beans + Tomatoes (see page 38) and Chocolate Orange Mousse (see page 176).

Protein + Fibre Cheat Sheet

A quick-glance guide to how much protein and fibre your favourite foods pack. I firmly stand against obsessing over numbers, but I do believe it helps to be educated in knowing roughly what you're working with. Whether you're building a bowl, making breakfast, or planning a snack, this page shows you the average protein content of common ingredients – so you can mix and match for meals that tick both the flavour and nutrition boxes.

WHAT DOES 20 G PROTEIN LOOK LIKE?

3 LARGE/US EXTRA-LARGE EGGS

100 G/3½ OZ CHICKEN

170 G/6 OZ FAT-FREE YOGURT

80 G/6½ OZ TOFU

250 G/9 OZ COOKED LENTILS

PLANT PROTEINS *Ingredient (per 100 g cooked unless stated)*	PROTEIN	FIBRE
Lentils	8 g	9 g
Chickpeas/garbanzo beans	7 g	8 g
Black beans	8 g	8 g
Butter/lima beans + cannellini beans	6 g	7 g
Kidney beans	6.5 g	8 g
Edamame (soybeans)	5 g	11 g
Tempeh	5 g	18 g
Firm tofu	1 g	13 g
Silken tofu	0 g	7 g
Lentil pasta (cooked)	8–10 g	15 g

ANIMAL PROTEINS *Ingredient (cooked unless stated)*	PROTEIN	FIBRE
Chicken breast (skinless)	31 g	0 g
Turkey breast	29 g	0 g
Chicken thigh	26 g	0 g
Salmon fillet	24 g	0 g
Tuna steak	29 g	0 g
White fish (cod/haddock/sea bass)	22 g	0 g
Prawns/shrimp	20 g	0 g
Smoked mackerel	25 g	0 g
Canned tuna	23 g	0 g
Canned sardines	21 g	0 g
Canned mackerel	20 g	0 g
Eggs (2 medium/US large eggs)	11–13 g	0 g
Halloumi	21 g	0 g

EVERYDAY ADD INS	PROTEIN	FIBRE
Wholemeal/whole wheat pasta	6 g	4 g
Soba noodles	5 g	3 g
Brown rice	2.5 g	1.8 g
Other grains (quinoa, barley, bulgur, couscous)	3–4 g	2–6 g
Rolled oats	13 g	10 g
Fat-free Greek yogurt or Skyr	10 g	0 g
Soy yogurt (Greek-style)	6 g	1.5 g
Cottage cheese	12 g	12 g
Cheddar or Parmesan	25 g	25 g
Nutritional yeast	47 g	0 g
Feta	14 g	0 g
Cream cheese	6 g	0 g
Soy milk	3.3 g	0 g
Skimmed milk	3.4 g	0 g
Whole nuts (peanuts, almonds, cashews, walnuts, pistachios)	5–7 g	1–3 g
Nut butters (peanut, almond)	25 g	6 g
Tahini	20 g	10 g
Seeds (chia, hemp, pumpkin, sunflower)	6–9 g	2–10 g
Cacao powder	20 g	30 g
Miso paste	11 g	5 g

QUICK WINS

- **Sprinkle nutritional yeast on bowls** (it adds a savoury, cheesy note)
- **Swap your normal milk** to soy or skimmed milk
- **Add low-fat dairy or blended silken tofu** to sauces
- **Sprinkle seeds** in and on everything

Healthyish

Breakfast + Brunch

Breakfast sets the tone for my entire day.

So, it needs to be worth getting out of bed for. These recipes are exactly that – flavoursome, packed with protein and fibre, and they have you covered whether you're sprinting out the door with a coffee or easing into a slow, cosy brunch. Some are quick, lots are preppable, all are delicious.

Makes 6 fritters | Prep 15 minutes | Cook 15 minutes

Halloumi + Veg Rostis with Harissa

V
DF/O
GF

Some mornings call for something hot, crispy and a little indulgent – and these rostis totally deliver. They tick both the veg and protein boxes without skimping on satisfaction, with salty halloumi, sweet carrot, courgette and a golden fried egg on top. Perfect for slow weekend mornings, but quick enough for weekdays too.

- 300 g/10½ oz potatoes
- 60 g/2¼ oz halloumi
- 50 g/1¾ oz carrot
- 100 g/3½ oz courgette/zucchini
- ½ tsp dried rosemary
- ½ tsp onion granules
- ½ tsp garlic granules
- 1 tsp dried oregano
- 2 large/US extra-large eggs
- 50 g/1¾ oz/scant ¼ cup fat-free Greek yogurt (DF: soy yogurt)
- 1 tsp harissa paste
- salt and pepper
- olive or avocado oil, for cooking
- a handful of salad leaves, to serve
- lemon wedges, to serve

1. Grate the potatoes (no need to peel), halloumi, carrot and courgette on the coarse side of a box grater. Place the grated mixture onto a clean tea/dish towel or double layer of kitchen paper/paper towels, gather up the sides and squeeze out as much water as you can. This helps the rostis get nice and crispy.

2. Transfer the mixture into a bowl and season with the rosemary, onion granules, garlic granules, oregano and a good pinch of salt and pepper. Mix well to combine.

3. Heat 1 tablespoon of oil in a large non-stick frying pan/skillet over medium heat. Spoon three mounds of the mixture into the pan and flatten each one with a spatula. Cook for 3–4 minutes per side, or until golden and crisp. Transfer to a plate and repeat with the remaining mixture, adding another tablespoon of oil to the pan.

4. Meanwhile, heat a drizzle of oil in a separate frying pan (or reuse the first once it's free) and fry the eggs until the whites are set and the edges are crisping up. Season with salt and pepper.

5. To serve, swipe the yogurt onto plates and swirl through the harissa. Stack the rostis on top, then crown with a fried egg, and add the salad leaves and a wedge of lemon to serve.

Future you:

- Cool and place rostis in an airtight container, storing in the fridge for up to 3 days.
- Cool and insert a piece of parchment paper between each rosti. Stack and freeze for up to 2 months.
- Thaw in the fridge overnight, or in the microwave on low power.
- Re-crisp the rostis in a hot pan, or preheated oven or air fryer at 180°C fan/200°C/400°F/gas mark 6. Cook the eggs fresh.

Serves 2 | Prep 10 minutes | Cook 15 minutes

Super Greens + Beans Baked Eggs

V
DF/O
GF/O
NF/O

Weekend brunches are made for scooping straight from the pan with a hunk of bread, and this pesto-ish number is an absolute winner. Between the eggs, butter beans and all the hidden greens, it's loaded with protein and fibre – the kind of brekkie that will actually keep you full past midday. You can cook this brunch entirely on the hob, or finish it off in the oven. Personally, I prefer the latter for perfect runny yolks, but both work well.

- 1 small head broccoli, cut into florets
- 1 x 400-g/14-oz can butter beans/lima beans
- 4 eggs
- 2 tbsp thick 0–5% fat yogurt (DF: soy yogurt)
- 1 tsp crispy chilli oil/crispy chile oil
- 2 slices seeded sourdough, toasted (GF: gluten-free bread)
- salt and pepper
- olive oil, for cooking

For the base

- 50 g/1¾ oz/1 scant cup baby spinach
- 50 g/1¾ oz/scant ½ cup frozen peas
- 15 g/½ oz/2 tbsp walnut halves (NF: pumpkin seeds)
- 1 garlic clove
- 20 g/¾ oz fresh basil
- 2 tbsp extra virgin olive oil
- juice of 1 lemon
- 20 g/¾ oz/¼ cup grated vegetarian Parmesan (DF: nutritional yeast)

1 If using the oven, preheat it to 180°C fan/200°C/400°F/gas mark 6 on the grill/broiler setting.

2 Add all the base ingredients to a food processor, season generously with salt and pepper and blitz until it looks like a loose, spoonable pesto; it should still have a little texture.

3 Heat a drizzle of olive oil in an ovenproof frying pan/skillet over medium heat. Add the broccoli with a pinch of salt and cook for 3–4 minutes until lightly charred and starting to soften. Turn the heat down slightly, then add the butter beans (along with a splash of the liquid from the can) and the green sauce. Stir and let everything gently simmer for 1–2 minutes.

4 Use the back of a spoon to create four small wells in the mixture. Crack an egg into each well. Cook on low heat on the hob or slide under the grill until the whites are set and the yolks are still runny; 6–8 minutes.

5 Finish with spoonfuls of yogurt and a drizzle of chilli oil. Serve straight from the pan with the toasted sourdough for dunking.

Future you:

Cool and place in an airtight container, storing in the fridge for up to 3 days.
Reheat the saucy base in the microwave until hot, or in a pan with a splash of water. For the eggs, either cook fresh ones or break up the old eggs and mix them in. Add the yogurt, chilli oil and toast fresh.

Serves 2 | Prep 10 minutes | Cook 10 minutes

Masala Omelette

GF

I must have eaten a masala omelette every other day during my four-week trip in India, and unsurprisingly never got bored. It's spicy, savoury and so delicious, and a brilliant way to switch up your usual breakfast. Serve simply alongside some leaves, or tuck it into a roti for a more substantial masala egg wrap.

- 6 eggs
- ½ tsp ground coriander
- ½ tsp ground cumin
- ½ tsp ground turmeric
- ½ onion, finely diced
- 1 garlic clove, minced
- 1 salad tomato, finely diced
- 1 green chilli/chile, thinly sliced
- 1 tbsp roughly chopped fresh coriander/cilantro
- salt and pepper
- olive oil, for cooking
- dressed salad leaves, to serve

1. Crack the eggs into a mixing bowl and add the ground coriander, cumin, turmeric and a generous pinch of salt and pepper. Whisk until the yolks and whites are completely combined.
2. Fold in the onion, garlic, tomato, green chilli and fresh coriander so everything is evenly distributed.
3. Heat a drizzle of oil in a non-stick frying pan/skillet over medium heat. Once hot, pour in half the egg mixture and use a spatula to spread it gently to the edges of the pan. Cook for about 3 minutes until the underside is golden and the top is mostly set, then flip and cook for another couple of minutes. Slide onto a plate.
4. Wipe out the pan, add another drizzle of oil and repeat with the rest of the egg mixture to make your second omelette. (Or, if you're working to the clock, cook both at once using two pans.)
5. Serve warm with dressed leaves.

Future you:

Cool and place in an airtight container, storing in the fridge for up to 2 days.
Enjoy cold, or reheat gently in a pan or the microwave until warmed through.

Serves 3 | Prep 10 minutes | Cook 30 minutes

Herby Smoked Salmon Egg Bake + Potatoes

This one's got all the makings of a café classic – but it's way easier (and cheaper) to make at home. The egg bake is soft and herby, with pockets of cream cheese and salty smoked salmon in every bite. A plateful that just so happens to pack in 30 g of protein, too.

baking sheet, lined
20-cm/8-in square baking dish, lined

- 6 eggs
- 100 g/3½ oz/scant ½ cup cottage cheese (DF: omit)
- 2 spring onions/scallions, finely chopped
- 1 tbsp finely chopped fresh dill
- 1 tbsp finely chopped fresh parsley
- juice of ½ lemon
- 100 g/3½ oz smoked salmon
- 50 g/1¾oz/scant ¼ cup light cream cheese (DF: dairy-free alternative)
- salt and pepper
- olive oil, for cooking
- rocket/arugula, to serve
- lemon wedges, to serve

For the potatoes

- 500 g/1 lb 2 oz potatoes, cut into 1-cm/½-in cubes
- ½ tsp garlic powder
- ½ tsp onion powder
- ½ tsp smoked paprika

1. Preheat the oven to 200°C fan/220°C/425°F/gas mark 7.

2. For the potatoes, spread the diced potato over the lined baking sheet. Drizzle with olive oil and sprinkle over the garlic powder, onion powder, smoked paprika and a pinch of salt and pepper. Toss well so every piece is coated, then roast for 25–30 minutes, turning halfway, until golden and crisp.

3. While the potatoes cook, crack the eggs into a mixing bowl and whisk until completely smooth. Stir in the cottage cheese, spring onion, dill, parsley, lemon juice and a generous pinch of salt and pepper.

4. Pour the egg mixture into the lined baking dish, then tear the smoked salmon into bite-sized pieces and scatter over the top, gently pressing a few pieces down so they're dotted throughout. Add the cream cheese in small spoonfuls across the surface.

5. Bake for 20–22 minutes until the centre is just set and the top is lightly golden.

6. Let it cool for a minute or two before slicing. Serve with the crispy potatoes, a handful of rocket and lemon wedges.

Future you:

- Cool and place in an airtight container, storing in the fridge for up to 3 days.
- Cool and freeze for up to 2 months.
- Thaw in the fridge overnight.
- Reheat the egg bake in the microwave for 1–2 minutes. Reheat the potatoes in an oven or air fryer to re-crisp.

Serves 2 | Prep 10 minutes | Cook 20–25 minutes

150 g/5¼ oz mushrooms, sliced
½ tsp garlic granules
50 g/1¾ oz/1 scant cup baby spinach
2 salad tomatoes, halved
2 slices seeded sourdough, toasted (GF: gluten-free bread)
1 avocado, sliced
salt and pepper
olive oil, for cooking

For the beans

¼ red onion, finely diced
1 garlic clove, minced
½ tsp dried oregano
¼ tsp chilli flakes/chile flakes
1 x 400-g/14-oz can cannellini beans
2–3 tbsp tomato purée/paste
2 tsp soy sauce (GF: tamari)
1 tsp maple syrup
30 g/1 oz/⅓ cup grated mature cheddar (VE: 2 tbsp nutritional yeast)

For the vegan version

1 x 300-g/10½-oz block extra-firm smoked tofu
100 ml/3½ fl oz/6½ tbsp dairy-free milk
1 tsp garlic granules
1 tsp onion granules
½ tsp ground turmeric
½ tsp ground cumin
1 tbsp nutritional yeast
1 tbsp dairy-free cream cheese
1 tbsp dairy-free pesto

For the vegetarian version

2 eggs

Power Breakfast: Two Ways

V

GF/O

Everyone loves a full brekkie, and this one's a proper satisfying plate that's big on colour, fibre and flavour. I've given you two routes, depending on what you fancy or who you're cooking for: one with very delicious pesto-scrambled tofu, the other with classic eggs. Pick your fighter and tuck in.

1 Start by making the beans. Heat a drizzle of olive oil in a saucepan over medium heat. Add the onion and garlic and cook for 3–4 minutes until softened. Stir in the oregano, chilli flakes, cannellini beans (with a splash of their liquid), tomato purée, soy sauce and maple syrup. Add the cheddar or nutritional yeast, plus a splash of water to loosen, then season with salt and pepper to taste. Turn the heat to low and let it simmer for around 10 minutes until thick and saucy.

2 Meanwhile, heat another drizzle of oil in a frying pan/skillet over medium heat. Add the mushrooms with the garlic granules and a pinch of salt. Cook for 4–5 minutes until golden, then add the spinach and cook for 1–2 minutes until just wilted. Set aside.

3 Place the tomato halves in the same pan, cut-side down, and cook for 2–3 minutes until softened and lightly caramelized. Set aside.

4 If using eggs, cook them to your liking (see page 10; I like mine fried).

5 For the vegan version, crumble the tofu into the same pan and cook for 1–2 minutes. In a small bowl, whisk together the milk, garlic granules, onion granules, turmeric, cumin and nutritional yeast. Pour into the pan and stir for 2–3 minutes until thickened. Stir in the cream cheese and pesto, and season to taste.

6 Build your breakfast plates with the beans, greens, tomatoes, eggs or tofu, toasted sourdough and sliced avocado.

Future you:

- Cool and place in an airtight container, storing in the fridge for up to 3 days.
- Cool and freeze the tofu scramble and beans for up to 2 months.
- Thaw in the fridge overnight, or in the microwave on low power.
- Reheat the tofu and beans in a pan or microwave with a splash of water, if necessary. Prepare the other elements fresh.

V/O
28.1g PROTEIN
15.5g FIBRE
VE/O
35.8g PROTEIN
15.5g FIBRE

Vanilla, Cardamom + Apricot Granola

V
VE/O

DF
GF
N

This is one of those back-pocket recipes I come back to time and time again. It's got crunch, clusters and just the right amount of sweetness, with cardamom and chewy apricots making it feel a little bit special and setting it apart from granola you can buy at the shops. Use the nuts and seeds below as a guide, swapping anything you don't have or like.

large baking sheet, lined

- 60 g/2¼ oz egg whites (about 2 large/US extra-large eggs) (VE: omit)
- 250 g/9 oz/3 cups rolled oats (GF: check label)
- 40 g/1½ oz/⅓ cup almonds, roughly chopped
- 40 g/1½ oz/⅓ cup cashews, roughly chopped
- 20 g/¾ oz/2½ tbsp sunflower seeds
- 25 g/1 oz/3 tbsp pumpkin seeds
- 20 g/¾ oz/3 tbsp hemp seeds
- 20 g/¾ oz/4 tsp chia seeds
- 1 tsp ground cardamom
- ½ tsp ground cinnamon
- ½ tsp fine sea salt
- 90 ml/3 fl oz/6 tbsp maple syrup or honey
- 2 tbsp coconut oil, melted
- 2 tsp vanilla extract
- 50 g/1¾ oz/⅓ cup dried apricots, finely chopped

1. Preheat the oven to 170°C fan/190°C/375°F/gas mark 5.
2. In a small bowl, whisk the egg whites for about 1 minute until light and frothy. Set aside.
3. In a large bowl, combine the oats, chopped nuts, seeds, cardamom, cinnamon and salt. Set aside.
4. In a jug or small bowl, whisk together the maple syrup or honey, coconut oil, vanilla and egg whites. Pour over the dry ingredients and stir until everything is evenly coated.
5. Spread the granola onto the lined baking sheet (use two if needed) and press it down lightly with the back of a spoon to help it form clusters.
6. Bake for 20 minutes, then gently turn sections over with a spatula, keeping the clusters intact. Return to the oven for another 10 minutes, or until golden.
7. Leave to cool completely on the baking sheet – it will crisp up further as it cools. Once cool, stir through the chopped apricots.

6.8g PROTEIN

5.1g FIBRE

Future you:

- Store in an airtight container in a cool, dry place for up to 2 weeks (or in the fridge for extra crunch).
- Freeze for up to 3 months.
- Thaw at room temperature for 15 minutes. If it has lost some crunch, you can briefly warm it in the oven.

Serves 2 | Prep 15 minutes | Cook 20 minutes

Huevos Rancheros

V
DF/O
GF/O

A non-traditional take on the classic Mexican breakfast that's every bit as satisfying. Huevos rancheros already tick all the boxes – protein, fibre and flavour – but I've given it a little extra boost with homemade refried beans and salsa. Everything comes together fast, and you can keep the toppings as minimal or as extra as you like.

- 4 small tortillas (GF: corn tortillas)
- 4 eggs
- ½ avocado, sliced
- 20 g/¾ oz feta (DF: dairy-free cheese or omit)
- salt and pepper
- olive oil, for cooking

For the salsa

- 4 salad tomatoes
- ½ onion, finely diced
- 1 garlic clove, minced
- 15 g/½ oz jarred sliced jalapeños, finely chopped
- ½ tsp chipotle paste (optional)
- juice of ½ lime
- 1 tbsp finely chopped fresh coriander/cilantro

For the refried beans

- ½ onion, finely chopped
- ¼ tsp ground cumin
- 1 x 400-g/14-oz can black beans, drained and rinsed
- juice of ½ lime

1 Start with the salsa. Finely chop the tomatoes by hand until almost a rough pulp. Heat a drizzle of olive oil in a small frying pan/skillet over medium heat. Add the onion and cook for 2–3 minutes until softened. Stir in the garlic, tomatoes, jalapeños, chipotle paste (if using), lime juice and a generous pinch of salt and pepper. Simmer gently for 8–10 minutes, stirring occasionally, until thick and jammy. Stir through the coriander, then set aside.

2 For the beans, heat a drizzle of oil in a small saucepan over medium heat. Add the onion and a pinch of salt and cook for 3–4 minutes until softened. Add in the cumin and cook for 30 seconds until fragrant. Tip in the black beans and 70 ml/2½ fl oz/5 tablespoons of water, then cover and cook for 5 minutes. Uncover and roughly mash half of the beans, then cook for another 2–3 minutes until thickened. Stir in the lime juice and season to taste.

3 Heat a non-stick frying pan over medium–high heat and warm the tortillas for 60 seconds on each side until lightly charred. Set aside.

4 In the same pan, cook the eggs to your liking (see page 10) – sunny-side up with a runny yolk works beautifully here.

5 To serve, layer each tortilla with a generous spoonful of beans, then add an egg, salsa, avocado slices and a crumble of feta.

Future you:

Best made to order. However, you can cool and place the beans in an airtight container and store in the fridge for up to 3 days.
Cool and freeze the beans for up to 2 months.
Thaw in the fridge overnight, or in the microwave on low power.
Reheat the beans in a pan or microwave with a splash of water, if needed. Make the salsa, cook the eggs and warm the tortillas fresh.

Serves 2 | Prep 10 minutes | Cook 18 minutes

Peaches + Cream Crumpet Bake

V

DF/O

GF/O

NF/O

It should be no surprise by now that I love a breakfast that feels indulgent but secretly does you good. Hello, crumpet bake. Crumpets are unbeatable at soaking up flavour, and here they turn golden on top and soft underneath – like a lighter take on bread-and-butter pudding that's just as good warm from the oven as it is reheated.

23 x 15-cm/9 x 6-in baking dish, lightly greased

- 1 small ripe banana
- 1 large/US extra-large egg
- 2 tbsp milk of choice
- ½ tsp ground cinnamon
- ½ tbsp maple syrup, plus extra to serve
- 4 crumpets (GF: gluten-free bread)
- 1 ripe peach
- 50 g/1¾ oz/¼ cup frozen blueberries
- 8 g/¼ oz/1 tbsp mixed seeds

To serve

- 100 g/3½ oz/scant ½ cup thick 0–5% fat yogurt (DF: soy yogurt)
- 1 tbsp peanut butter (NF: tahini)
- a splash of maple syrup (optional)

1. Preheat the oven to 180°C fan/200°C/400°F/gas mark 6.
2. In a blender or small bowl, blend or whisk together the banana, egg, milk, cinnamon and maple syrup until smooth.
3. Tear or chop the crumpets into bite-sized pieces and place them in the greased baking dish. Pour over the banana mixture and gently stir to coat every piece. Leave to soak for 5 minutes.
4. Meanwhile, core and thinly slice the peach.
5. Fold the blueberries and peach slices through the soaked crumpets, then scatter the mixed seeds over the top.
6. Bake for about 18 minutes, or until set and golden on the surface with a few crisp edges.
7. Serve warm with the yogurt and a drizzle of peanut butter. Add a splash of maple syrup, if you like a little extra sweetness.

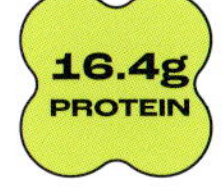

Future you:

Cool and place in an airtight container, storing in the fridge for up to 3 days.

Reheat in the microwave for 1–2 minutes, or in the oven at 160°C fan/180°C/350°F/gas mark 4 for 8–10 minutes until heated through. Add the toppings fresh.

Serves 1 | Prep 5 minutes | Cook 6 minutes

Scrambled Oats

V

NF/O

A properly good speedy breakfast that's somewhere between porridge, pancakes and granola. Scrambled oats – or frying pan granola, as I like to call it – are made by cooking an oat batter until golden, then breaking it into clusters. It's high in fibre and a good source of protein, endlessly adaptable, and a brilliant way to use up overripe bananas or switch up your usual oats.

- 1 small ripe banana, plus extra to serve
- 1 small/US medium egg
- 50 g/1¾ oz/generous ½ cup rolled oats (GF: check label)
- 1 tsp ground cinnamon
- pinch of salt
- 1 tsp coconut oil
- 150 g/5¼ oz/scant ¾ cup thick 0–5% fat yogurt (DF: soy yogurt)
- 50 g/1¾ oz/¼ cup frozen raspberries
- ½ tsp cacao nibs (optional)
- 1 tsp flaked/slivered almonds (NF: pumpkin seeds)

1. Mash the banana in a bowl with a fork until smooth. Add the egg and whisk well. Stir in the oats, cinnamon and a pinch of salt to form a thick batter.
2. Heat the coconut oil in a non-stick frying pan/skillet over medium heat. Pour in the batter and gently spread it out into a thin pancake. Let it cook undisturbed for about 1 minute until the underside begins to set, then use a spatula to start breaking it up into rough clusters. Keep cooking and stirring for another 4–5 minutes until the pieces are golden and crisp in places.
3. Serve straight away with the yogurt, raspberries and extra banana. Finish with the cacao nibs and flaked almonds – or any other toppings you fancy.

Future you:

Cool and place in an airtight container, storing in the fridge for up to 2 days. For best results, reheat briefly in the oven or an air fryer to re-crisp. If you don't mind a softer texture, pop in the microwave for a minute to warm through.

Serves 4 | Prep 10 minutes | Cook 20 minutes

Silken Beans + Tomatoes

V

VE/O

DF

GF/O

This one ticks all the boxes: creamy, comforting, nourishing and made almost entirely from cans and pantry bits. The silken tofu (don't knock it till you try it!) gives the beans a glossy, velvety texture without any dairy, and the sun-dried tomato drizzle adds a gorgeous salty-savoury punch on top.

- 400 g/14 oz cherry tomatoes on the vine
- 2 tsp extra virgin olive oil
- ½ tsp dried oregano
- ½ tsp chilli flakes/chile flakes
- 4 eggs (VE: omit)
- 4 slices sourdough, toasted (GF: gluten-free bread)
- salt and pepper
- olive oil, for cooking

For the silken beans

- 1 x 300-g/10½-oz block silken tofu
- 1 garlic clove
- juice of 1 lemon
- 2 tbsp extra virgin olive oil
- 2 x 400-g/14-oz cans cannellini beans, drained
- 1 tsp miso paste
- 3 tbsp nutritional yeast

For the drizzle

- 10 jarred sun-dried tomatoes, plus 3 tbsp oil from the jar
- 1 garlic clove
- 1 tbsp nutritional yeast
- 1 tbsp chopped fresh basil, plus extra to serve

1. Preheat the oven to 200°C fan/220°C/425°F/gas mark 7.
2. Place the tomatoes in an ovenproof dish. Drizzle with the oil and sprinkle with the oregano, chilli flakes and a good pinch of salt and pepper. Roast for 15 minutes until soft and blistered.
3. Meanwhile, make the beans. Add the silken tofu, garlic, lemon juice and olive oil to a blender and blitz until completely smooth. Tip the mixture into a large frying pan/skillet over medium heat. Stir in the drained cannellini beans, miso paste and nutritional yeast. Season generously, then turn the heat down to low and let it gently bubble for around 10 minutes until thick and creamy.
4. For the drizzle, blitz everything together in a small blender or food processor until smooth, adding a splash of water to loosen, if needed.
5. Heat a drizzle of oil in another frying pan over medium heat and cook the eggs to your liking (see page 10).
6. Spoon the silken beans into bowls, add the roasted tomatoes and top with the fried egg. Finish with a generous drizzle of the sun-dried tomato sauce, some extra fresh basil and the toasted bread for mopping.

Future you:

- Cool and place in an airtight container, storing in the fridge for up to 3 days.
- Cool and freeze the beans and drizzle for up to 2 months.
- Thaw in the fridge overnight.
- Reheat the beans in a pan or microwave with a splash of water. Add everything else fresh.

Serves 4 | Prep 10 minutes | Cook 20–22 minutes

Smoked Salmon + Egg Tarts

These tarts look impressive but couldn't be simpler to make – perfect for brunch with family, a weekend breakfast spread or even a quick lunch. The secret is baking the pastry twice so it stays crisp under the toppings.

large baking sheet, lined

- 1 x 320-g/11-oz sheet puff pastry (GF: gluten-free puff pastry)
- 1 egg, beaten
- sprinkle of sesame seeds
- 50 g/1¾ oz/1 scant cup baby spinach
- 100 g/3½ oz/scant ½ cup light cream cheese (DF: dairy-free alternative)
- 4 eggs
- 100 g/3½ oz smoked salmon
- a handful of chives, finely chopped
- salt and pepper
- dressed salad leaves, to serve

1. Preheat the oven to 200°C fan/220°C/425°F/gas mark 7.
2. Unroll the puff pastry and cut it into four equal rectangles. Using a small knife, score a border about 2 cm/¾ in from the edge of each rectangle (don't cut all the way through), then prick the centre a few times with a fork so it doesn't puff up too much. Brush the borders with the beaten egg and scatter over a few sesame seeds, along with a pinch of salt and pepper.
3. Bake for about 10 minutes until slightly golden and puffed up. As soon as they come out, press down the centre of each tart with the back of a spoon to make a little well for the fillings.
4. Meanwhile, cook the spinach in the microwave for 30 seconds until wilted, then squeeze out any excess water with a piece of kitchen paper/paper towel.
5. Spread a layer of cream cheese over each tart base – don't worry if the pastry flakes slightly, just patch it together as you go. Season lightly with salt and pepper, then arrange the wilted spinach around the edges of each well, leaving a space in the middle for the egg.
6. Crack an egg into each tart. Carefully slide them back into the oven for 10–12 minutes, or until the whites are just set but the yolks are still runny.
7. Once baked, top with slices of smoked salmon and a scattering of fresh chives. Serve alongside dressed salad leaves.

Future you:

Cool and place in an airtight container, storing in the fridge for up to 2 days

Reheat in a hot oven for 5–7 minutes, or enjoy at room temperature.

Serves 1 | Prep 5 minutes | Chill 4 hours or overnight

Matcha + Strawberry Chia Pudding

V
VE/O
DF/O

GF/O

I love this flavour combination for breakfast, especially as you get a subtle caffeine boost from the earthy matcha to kick start the day. If you're anti-chia (it's okay, I get it!), try blending the chia seeds with the milk before chilling; it gives a smoother, more pudding-like texture that might just win you over.

- 80 ml/2¾ fl oz/⅓ cup milk of choice
- 150 g/5¼ oz/scant ¾ cup fat-free thick yogurt (DF/VE: soy yogurt)
- 1 tbsp maple syrup, plus extra if you like it sweeter
- ¼ tsp vanilla extract
- 1 tsp matcha powder
- 20 g/¾ oz/4 tsp chia seeds

To serve

- 2–3 strawberries, hulled and finely diced
- granola (see Vanilla, Cardamom and Apricot Granola, page 30, or use store-bought) (GF: gluten-free granola)

1 In a mixing bowl, whisk together the milk, yogurt, maple syrup, vanilla extract and matcha powder until smooth and no lumps remain. Stir in the chia seeds and mix well.

2 Pour the mixture into an airtight jar or container, then seal and refrigerate for at least 4 hours, or overnight, until thickened.

3 When ready to serve, give the pudding a quick stir and top with fresh strawberries and a handful of granola. You can serve with an extra dollop of yogurt too, if you like.

Future you:

Cool and place in an airtight container, storing in the fridge for up to 3 days.

On-the-go Lunches

Lunch is the meal I always forget to plan.

This means I either end up scavenging the fridge and throwing together some very questionable pairings, or paying a lot of money for something I didn't even want. Well, good job someone has developed these recipes to save us. They're packable, preppable and high in protein, so you stay full and smug. Make once, enjoy for days. Trust me – the efficiency tastes very good.

Serves 4 | Prep 15 minutes | Cook 15 minutes

Stuff Me: Crunchy Dill Chicken Salad

Over the next few pages you'll find my 'Stuff Me' fillings – recipes designed to be packed into whatever vessel you fancy, from wraps and bagels to baked potatoes or crisp lettuce cups. This crunchy dill chicken salad is a strong contender for my favourite. Creamy, herby and full of texture thanks to a handful of seeds, it's a fridge hero for busy weekdays. Add a splash of pickle brine if you like things punchy.

- 400 g/14 oz chicken breasts
- 50 g/1¾ oz/3½ tbsp good-quality mayonnaise
- 100 g/3½ oz/scant ½ cup thick 0–5% fat yogurt (DF: soy yogurt)
- 1 tsp Dijon mustard
- 2 dill pickles, finely chopped
- ¼ red onion, finely diced
- ⅓ cucumber, finely diced and patted dry
- 15 g/½ oz/2 tbsp sunflower seeds, toasted
- 1 tbsp finely chopped fresh dill
- 1 tbsp finely chopped fresh parsley
- salt and pepper
- olive oil, for cooking

1. Heat a glug of olive oil in a lidded frying pan/skillet over medium–high heat. Add the chicken breasts and sear for about 3 minutes on each side until lightly golden.
2. Pour in enough water to come about 2 cm/¾ in up the sides of the pan. Cover with a lid and let the chicken steam for 10 minutes, or until fully cooked through.
3. Transfer the cooked chicken to a chopping board and shred either by using two forks, or by placing it in a mixing bowl and using a hand mixer. The latter method is quicker, but leads to more washing up – I'll leave the choice with you!
4. In a large mixing bowl, stir together the mayo, yogurt, Dijon mustard and a generous pinch of salt and pepper. Add the shredded chicken, pickles, red onion and cucumber. Fold everything together until coated, then stir through the toasted sunflower seeds and herbs. Taste and adjust the seasoning.

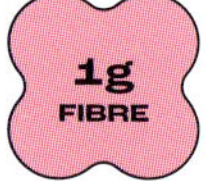

Future you:

Cool and place in an airtight container, storing in the fridge for up to 3 days.

Serves 4 Prep 15 minutes

Stuff Me: Mediterranean Tuna Smash

The 'Stuff Me' series continues with a proper fridge favourite. This tuna smash is part Mediterranean salad, part smashed avo, with a bit of extra protein from the beans and eggs. Pile it on toast, or stuff it into a wrap, sandwich or baked potato for a quick, high-protein lunch.

- 2 large/US extra-large eggs
- 1 small avocado, mashed
- 200 g/7 oz cannellini beans, drained and rinsed
- 2 x 120-g/4-oz cans tuna, drained
- 1 small red (bell) pepper, finely diced
- 2 spring onions/scallions, thinly sliced
- 40 g/1½ oz feta, crumbled
- 1 tbsp chopped olives or capers
- juice of ½ lemon
- 15 g/½ oz fresh basil, roughly torn
- salt and pepper
- olive oil, to serve

1. Bring a small pot of water to boil. Gently lower in the eggs and boil them for exactly 9 minutes (set a timer!). Drain and run under cold water until cool enough to handle, then peel and roughly chop into small pieces. Set aside.
2. In a large bowl, mash the avocado and cannellini beans together with a fork until mostly smooth but still with some texture.
3. Add the tuna, chopped eggs, red pepper, spring onion, feta, olives or capers and lemon juice. Stir in the basil. Season with black pepper and a small pinch of salt – the feta and olives are salty already, so you shouldn't need too much. If the mixture feels a little dry, add a drizzle of olive oil to bring it all together.

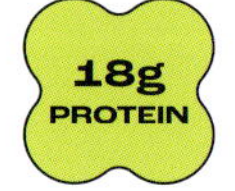

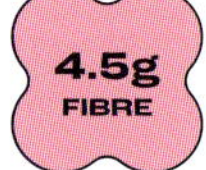

Future you:

Cool and place in an airtight container, storing in the fridge for up to 3 days.

Stuff Me: Chickpea Salad

GF

The 'Stuff Me' finale, and proof that a plant-based filling can still hit all the right notes. Silken tofu makes it rich and satisfying, chickpeas add the chew, and quick-pickled onions bring the zing. Feel free to mix things up: swap the celery for cucumber if that's more your vibe, or toss in whatever herbs you've got lying around.

- 2 x 400-g/14-oz cans chickpeas/garbanzo beans, drained and rinsed
- 1 x 300-g/10½-oz block silken tofu
- 1 tsp Dijon mustard
- 1 tsp white or apple cider vinegar
- 1 tsp tahini
- 2 tbsp nutritional yeast
- 2 sticks/stalks celery, finely chopped
- 1 tbsp finely chopped fresh dill
- salt and pepper

For the quick-pickled onion

- ½ small red onion, thinly sliced
- 1 tbsp white or apple cider vinegar

1 Start by quick-pickling the onion. Place the sliced onion in a small bowl or jar. Add the vinegar, 1 tablespoon of water and a pinch of salt, then scrunch it together with your fingers to help it soften. Set aside to pickle lightly – it'll be ready by the time you serve.

2 Roughly mash the chickpeas in a large bowl with a fork or potato masher, leaving a few whole for texture. Set aside.

3 In a blender, combine the silken tofu, mustard, vinegar, tahini and nutritional yeast. Blend until smooth and creamy.

4 Add the blended mixture to the mashed chickpeas, along with the celery and dill. Fold everything together until well combined.

5 Finally, stir through the pickled onions and season generously with salt and pepper. Taste and adjust the seasoning as needed – a splash more vinegar or mustard will brighten it up if it needs it.

Future you:

Cool and place in an airtight container, storing in the fridge for up to 3 days.

Serves 4–5 | Prep 15 minutes | Cook 18 minutes

Corn + Kale Pasta Salad

There will be no sad desk lunches on my watch. This one has it all: charred corn, herbs and feta bring freshness, while kale and chicken make it properly satisfying, and a zippy dressing ties it all together. It tastes even better as the days go by, so do future you a favour and make a big batch.

- 2 corn on the cob
- 250 g/9 oz dried pasta of choice (GF: gluten-free pasta)
- 2 large chicken breasts, butterflied
- ½ tsp paprika
- ½ tsp dried thyme
- ½ tsp dried rosemary
- ¼ tsp chilli flakes/chile flakes
- ¼ tsp garlic granules
- ¼ tsp onion granules
- 50 g/1¾ oz kale leaves
- 2 spring onions/scallions, thinly sliced
- 1 tbsp finely chopped fresh parsley
- 100 g/3½ oz feta, crumbled (DF: dairy-free alternative)
- salt and pepper
- olive oil, for cooking

For the dressing

- 1 tbsp red wine vinegar
- 2 tbsp extra virgin olive oil
- 1 garlic clove, minced
- ½ tsp Dijon mustard

1 Heat a glug of oil in a large frying pan/skillet over medium heat. Add the corn and cook for about 8 minutes, turning occasionally, until tender and nicely charred. Lift out of the pan and set aside.

2 Meanwhile, cook the pasta in salted boiling water according to packet instructions until al dente. Drain, then rinse under cold water to stop the cooking and cool it down.

3 Season the butterflied chicken breasts with the paprika, thyme, rosemary, chilli flakes, garlic granules, onion granules and a good pinch of salt and pepper. Using the same pan as the corn, heat another drizzle of oil over medium heat and cook the chicken for about 4 minutes per side, or until golden and cooked through. Set aside to rest.

4 Add the kale to the same pan with a pinch of salt and pepper. Cook for 1–2 minutes until just wilted, then remove from the heat.

5 Whisk the dressing ingredients together in a small bowl or jar with a pinch of salt and pepper until smooth and emulsified.

6 Cut the kernels off the corn cobs and dice the chicken. Add both to a large bowl, along with the pasta, kale, spring onions, parsley and feta. Pour over the dressing and toss until everything is evenly coated, then serve.

Future you:

Cool and place in an airtight container, storing in the fridge for up to 4 days.

Serves 2 | Prep 20 minutes | Cook 10 minutes

Tempeh Rice Paper Rolls

V

GF/O

These are as fun to make as they are to eat. And once you've mastered the method, you'll be flying. The tempeh turns deliciously sticky, which gets beautifully balanced with the crisp vegetables and soft noodles. A proper texture and flavour sensation.

- 2 tbsp soy sauce (GF: tamari)
- 1 garlic clove, minced
- 2.5-cm/1-in piece fresh ginger, grated
- ½ tbsp toasted sesame oil
- 1 heaped tsp cornflour/cornstarch
- 1 tbsp maple syrup
- ½ tbsp rice vinegar
- 200 g/7 oz tempeh, cut into 1-cm/½-in cubes
- 1 x 50-g/1¾-oz nest vermicelli noodles
- 1 carrot, peeled and julienned
- 1 small cucumber, julienned
- ½ red (bell) pepper, thinly sliced
- 1 tbsp fresh coriander/cilantro leaves
- 1 spring onion/scallion, sliced into thin strips
- 6–8 rice paper sheets
- pepper
- olive oil, for frying

1. Add the soy sauce, garlic, ginger, sesame oil, cornflour, maple syrup, rice vinegar, 60 ml/2 fl oz/¼ cup of water and a pinch of pepper to a small jar. Seal and shake until smooth.

2. Heat a glug of oil in a frying pan/skillet over medium–high heat. Add the tempeh cubes and fry for 3–4 minutes until golden on all sides. Turn the heat down, pour in the sauce and stir for 30 seconds–1 minute until it thickens and coats the tempeh. Set aside to cool slightly.

3. Cook the vermicelli noodles according to packet instructions. Drain, rinse under cold water and set aside.

4. If you haven't already, prep all the vegetables so they're ready to go – carrot, cucumber, red pepper, coriander and spring onion.

5. Fill a wide shallow dish or pan with warm water. Dip one rice paper sheet into the water for 10–15 seconds until it just softens, then place it on a damp surface or board. Pile a small amount of noodles, tempeh and vegetables in the centre, then fold in the sides and roll tightly from the bottom up. Repeat with the remaining papers and filling, then serve.

Future you:

Cool and place in an airtight container, storing in the fridge for up to 2 days.

WRAPPER
MEKONG

Serves 2 | Prep 10 minutes | Cook 10 minutes

Mango, Avocado + Halloumi Salad With Aji Verde

V
VE/O

GF

If summer were a salad, it would look like this. Sweet mango, creamy avocado and golden halloumi all tangled up with a herby, spicy aji verde that brings everything to life. It's got crunch, colour and proper personality – the way a salad should be, if you ask me.

- 100 g/3½ oz/scant ½ cup thick 0–5% fat yogurt (DF/VE: soy yogurt)
- 10 g/¼ oz fresh coriander/cilantro
- 20 g/¾ oz jarred sliced jalapeños
- juice of 1 lime
- 1 tsp garlic granules
- 225 g/8 oz light halloumi, sliced (DF/VE: extra-firm tofu)
- 1 x 250-g/9-oz pouch cooked quinoa
- 1 x 200-g/7-oz can chickpeas/garbanzo beans, drained and rinsed
- 1 ripe mango, peeled and diced
- 1 ripe avocado, diced
- salt and pepper
- olive oil, for cooking
- a few sprigs of dill

1 Start by making the aji verde. Add the yogurt, coriander, jalapeños, lime juice, garlic granules, 2½ tablespoons of water and a pinch of salt and pepper to a blender. Blend until smooth, adding a splash more water if needed to reach a pourable consistency. Taste and adjust as needed; more lime for sharpness or extra jalapeños if you like heat.

2 Heat a drizzle of oil in a non-stick frying pan/skillet over medium heat. Add the halloumi slices and cook for 1–2 minutes on each side until golden and lightly crisp.

3 Microwave the quinoa pouch according to packet instructions, then tip it into a large mixing bowl. Add the chickpeas, mango and avocado, and toss gently to combine.

4 Divide the salad between plates, top with the golden halloumi and finish with a generous drizzle of the aji verde and scattering over a few sprigs of dill.

Future you:

- Cool and place in an airtight container, storing in the fridge for up to 3 days.
- ❄ Cool and freeze the quinoa and chickpeas for up to 3 months.
- Thaw in the fridge overnight.

Serves 2 | Prep 15 minutes | Cook 12–15 minutes

Smoked Mackerel Potato Salad

V/O

DF/O

Potato salad: but make it chic. It's smoky, herby and just the right amount of creamy, with shaved fennel for freshness and cannellini beans to bulk it out, while sneaking in a solid boost of protein and fibre – totalling 40 g and 17 g respectively per serving.

- 500 g/1 lb 2 oz baby potatoes
- 1 medium–large fennel bulb, thinly shaved
- 1 x 400 g/14-oz can cannellini beans, drained and rinsed
- 2 smoked mackerel fillets, skin removed and torn into chunks (V: hard-boiled eggs)
- 60 g/2¼ oz lamb's lettuce or watercress
- salt and pepper
- Parmesan, to serve (V: vegetarian Parmesan; DF: omit)

For the dressing

- 50 g/1¾ oz/scant ¼ cup thick 0–5% fat yogurt (DF: soy yogurt)
- 1 tbsp wholegrain mustard
- juice of ½ lemon
- 1 tsp honey
- 1 tbsp extra virgin olive oil
- 1 tbsp finely chopped fresh dill

1. Start with the potatoes. Halve any larger ones and place them in a pan of salted cold water. Bring to the boil and cook for 12–15 minutes, or until tender when pierced with a knife. Drain and set aside to cool slightly.
2. While the potatoes cook, make the dressing. In a small bowl, whisk together the yogurt, mustard, lemon juice, honey, olive oil, dill and 1 tablespoon of water until smooth. Season generously with salt and pepper to taste – it should be tangy to balance the rich mackerel.
3. While the potatoes are still warm, add them to a large bowl and spoon over half the dressing so they can absorb the flavour.
4. Once the potatoes have cooled to room temperature, add the fennel, cannellini beans, mackerel and lamb's lettuce. Drizzle over the remaining dressing and gently toss until everything is evenly coated.
5. Divide between plates and finish with a few shavings of Parmesan and a good grind of black pepper.

Future you:

Cool and place in an airtight container, storing in the fridge for up to 3 days.

Serves 2 | Prep 10 minutes | Cook 10 minutes

High-Protein Med Veg Ciabatta

GF/O

Of course this book wouldn't be complete without a loaded sammie, and this one's a standout. Crispy, lemony tofu, creamy pesto, tangy peppers and chewy sun-dried tomatoes, all tucked into a crusty ciabatta. It's the best of the Med between two slices of bread, and with over 40 g/1½ oz of protein and nearly 20 g/¾ oz of fibre, it's as nourishing as it is delicious.

- 1 small courgette/zucchini, thinly sliced lengthways
- 2 ciabatta rolls or 1 large ciabatta (GF: gluten-free alternative)
- 1 tsp basil pesto (DF/VE: dairy-free pesto)
- 1 tsp light cream cheese (DF/VE: dairy-free alternative)
- 2 jarred roasted red (bell) peppers, sliced
- 4 sun-dried tomatoes, roughly chopped
- a handful of rocket/arugula
- salt and pepper

For the herby tofu

- 300 g/10½ oz extra-firm smoked tofu, sliced into slabs 1-cm/½-in thick
- 1 tsp cornflour/cornstarch
- ½ tsp dried oregano
- ¼ tsp garlic granules
- ¼ tsp onion granules
- 1 tbsp extra virgin olive oil
- juice of ½ lemon

1. Start with the tofu. Pat it dry with kitchen paper/paper towel and cut into even slices. Add the cornflour, oregano, garlic and onion granules, olive oil, lemon juice and a good pinch of salt and pepper to a mixing bowl. Toss the tofu through until well coated.
2. Heat a non-stick frying pan/skillet over medium heat. Fry the tofu for 2–3 minutes on each side until golden and crisp at the edges. Transfer to a plate and set aside.
3. Add the courgette slices to the same pan and cook for 2–3 minutes per side until lightly charred and softened. Set aside on a plate.
4. Halve the ciabatta and toast it lightly. Stir the pesto and cream cheese together, then spread over the cut sides of the bread.
5. Layer on the courgette, roasted peppers, sun-dried tomatoes, rocket and crispy tofu. Top with the other half of the ciabatta, press down gently and cut in half to serve.

Future you:

Best eaten fresh, but can be refrigerated, if wrapped airtight, for up to 3 days.

Serves 2 | Prep 10 minutes | Cook 20 minutes

Two-Ingredient Bagels

DF/O

These are never going to rival a bakery bagel, but they come close. They're made from two simple ingredients, pack 13 g of protein each and are quick to make. I've given you the base recipe, plus my favourite filling combo of scrambled eggs, feta, dill and olives. Yum.

baking sheet, lined

- 125 g/4½ oz/scant 1 cup self-raising/self-rising flour, plus extra for dusting
- 130 g/4½ oz/generous ½ cup thick fat-free yogurt (DF: soy yogurt)
- ¼ tsp salt

For the topping

- 1 egg, beaten
- 1 tsp white sesame seeds
- ½ tsp black sesame seeds
- ½ tsp poppy seeds
- ½ tsp garlic granules
- ½ tsp onion granules
- ½ tsp flaky salt

For the filling

- 4 eggs
- 2 tsp olive oil spread
- 40 g/1½ oz feta, crumbled (DF: dairy-free cheese or omit)
- 80 g/2¾ oz/⅓ cup light cream cheese (DF: dairy-free cheese or omit)
- ½ tbsp finely chopped fresh dill
- 2 tbsp thinly sliced spring onion/scallion
- 6 pitted green olives, roughly chopped
- 2 sun-dried tomatoes, roughly chopped

Bagel alone:

With filling:

1. Preheat the oven to 180°C fan/200°C/400°F/gas mark 6.
2. In a bowl, mix the flour, yogurt and salt until it starts to come together. Tip onto a lightly floured surface and knead briefly until smooth. If it's too wet, dust with a little flour; if too dry, dampen your hands and keep kneading until the dough feels soft and pliable.
3. Divide the dough into two pieces. Roll each into a thin log, then bring the ends together to form a ring, pinching firmly to seal. Place on the lined baking sheet.
4. For the topping, brush with beaten egg wash and sprinkle generously with the remaining topping ingredients. Bake for 15–20 minutes until golden and risen.
5. Meanwhile, make the filling. Crack the eggs into a jug or bowl, season with salt and pepper and whisk until combined.
6. Heat the olive oil spread in a non-stick pan over medium-low heat. Add the eggs and cook gently, stirring occasionally, until softly set. Fold in half the feta and set aside.
7. In a small bowl, mix the cream cheese with the dill, spring onion and a pinch of salt and pepper.
8. Slice the warm bagels in half and spread the cream cheese thickly on both sides. Add the scrambled egg, then top with the olives, sun-dried tomatoes and remaining feta. Sandwich together and serve while warm.

Future you:

Place the bagels in an airtight container, storing in the fridge for up to 2 days.
Cool, slice in half, and freeze for up to 3 months.
Toast the bagels from chilled or frozen.

Snacks

I've accepted that I will always be someone who needs snacks.

So, rather than pretending I can survive the afternoon without them, I just started making snacks that actually do something. There's a mix of sweet and savoury here, all designed to keep you full, taste delicious and save you from the frantic cupboard forage. Keep them on hand and thank me later.

Serves 2 | Prep 10 minutes | Cook 5 minutes

Cottage Cheese Bruschetta

V
VE/O
DF/O
GF/O

Upping your protein doesn't always mean reinventing the wheel. Sometimes it's as simple as adding a protein boost to something you already love – like this bruschetta. It's every bit as delicious as the classic, just a lot more satisfying thanks to a generous layer of cottage cheese under those zingy chopped tomatoes.

- 2 slices sourdough (GF: gluten-free bread)
- 1 small garlic clove, halved
- 2 tomatoes, finely chopped
- ½ small shallot, finely chopped
- a small handful of finely chopped basil
- ½ tbsp extra virgin olive oil
- ½ tsp red wine vinegar
- 100 g/3½ oz/scant ½ cup cottage cheese (DF/VE: dairy-free cream cheese or whipped tofu)
- a drizzle of balsamic glaze (optional)
- salt and pepper
- olive oil, for cooking

1. Heat 1 teaspoon of olive oil in a frying pan/skillet over medium heat and toast the sourdough until golden on both sides. While still warm, rub one side with the cut side of the garlic clove.
2. In a small bowl, combine the tomato, shallot, basil, extra virgin olive oil, red wine vinegar and a generous pinch of salt and pepper.
3. Spread the cottage cheese onto the toast, then top with the tomato mixture. Drizzle with balsamic glaze, if using, and serve immediately.

Future you:

Best made fresh. The tomato topping can be made up to 1 day ahead and kept in the fridge.

Serves 1 | Prep 5 minutes | Cook 15 minutes

Magic Shell Protein Pot

V
VE/O
DF/O
GF
NF/O

Remember those chocolate-dipped ice creams that cracked when you bit into them? Well, this is the yogurt-pot version. Creamy, crunchy and high in protein, it comes together in minutes with just a handful of ingredients. A perfect mid-afternoon snack that tastes like a little dessert.

- 120 g/4 oz/generous ½ cup thick 0–5% fat yogurt (DF/VE: soy yogurt)
- ½ tbsp peanut butter (NF: tahini)
- 1 tsp honey (VE: maple syrup)
- 2–3 strawberries, finely diced
- 10 g/⅓ oz dark/bittersweet chocolate
- a pinch of flaky sea salt

1. Spoon the yogurt into a ramekin, small bowl or jar, then stir in the peanut butter and honey until smooth and creamy. Fold through the chopped strawberries.
2. Melt the chocolate in a microwave in 15-second bursts until just melted, then pour it over the yogurt mixture. Use the back of a spoon to spread it gently into an even layer.
3. Freeze for 15 minutes, or until the chocolate has fully hardened. Sprinkle over a pinch of flaky salt, then crack it open and dig in.

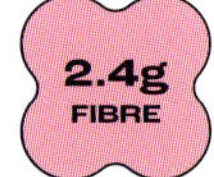

Future you:

Cool and place in an airtight container, storing in the fridge for up to 2 days.

Date + Tahini Loaf

V
VE/O

DF/O
NF/O

If banana bread had a Middle Eastern cousin, this would be it. Made with sweet dates, nutty tahini and a touch of cinnamon, it's soft, moist and packed full of flavour. It's also naturally sweetened and full of healthy fats, making it a brilliant afternoon pick-me-up with a cup of tea or coffee.

20 x 10-cm/8 x 4-in loaf tin/pan, lined

- 2 eggs (VE: mix 2 tbsp ground flaxseed/linseed with 5 tbsp water, and leave to rest for 5 minutes)
- 85 g/3 oz/¼ cup tahini
- 1 tsp vanilla extract
- 60 g/2¼ oz/generous ¼ cup thick 0–5% fat yogurt (DF/VE: soy yogurt)
- 60 g/2¼ oz/scant ¼ cup honey (VE: maple syrup)
- 80 ml/2¾ fl oz/⅓ cup milk of choice
- 200 g/7 oz/1⅔ cups plain/all-purpose flour
- 1 tsp bicarbonate of soda/baking soda
- ¼ tsp salt
- 1 tsp ground cinnamon
- 100 g/3½ oz/¾ cup pitted dates, finely chopped
- 30 g/1 oz/scant ¼ cup walnut halves, roughly chopped (NF: pumpkin seeds or omit)
- 1 tbsp sesame seeds

1. Preheat the oven to 170°C fan/190°C/375°F/gas mark 5.
2. In a large bowl, whisk together the eggs, tahini, vanilla, yogurt, honey and milk until smooth.
3. In another bowl, mix the flour, bicarbonate of soda, salt and cinnamon.
4. Add the dry ingredients to the wet and stir until just combined, then fold through the chopped dates and walnuts.
5. Pour the batter into the prepared tin and smooth the top. Sprinkle over the sesame seeds to create an even crust.
6. Bake for 40–45 minutes, or until a skewer inserted into the centre comes out clean.
7. Leave to cool in the tin for 10 minutes before turning out onto a wire rack to cool completely. Serve with a cup of tea and a smear of butter, if you like.

Future you:

- Cool and place in an airtight container, storing at room temperature for up to 3 days, or in the fridge for up to 6 days.
- Slice and freeze for up to 3 months.
- Toast straight from frozen or defrost overnight.
- Enjoy at room temperature, toasted, or warmed for 10 seconds in the microwave.

Serves 4 Prep 5 minutes Cook 35–40 minutes

Salt + Vinegar Snack Mix

VE
DF

This is my salt and vinegar crisp obsession, reimagined. All that tangy, salty goodness but in roasted snack form, with a much bigger hit of protein and fibre to keep you going.

large baking sheet, lined

- 1 x 400-g/14-oz can chickpeas/garbanzo beans, drained and rinsed
- 150 g/5¼ oz/generous 1 cup frozen edamame, thawed
- 1 tbsp olive oil
- 1 tbsp vinegar of choice (malt, white wine or apple cider work well)
- salt and pepper

1. Preheat the oven to 210°C fan/230°C/450°F/gas mark 8.
2. Thoroughly pat the chickpeas and edamame dry with a clean tea/dish towel – the drier they are, the crunchier they'll roast.
3. Spread them out on the lined baking sheet (no overlapping) and roast for 10 minutes to help them dry out.
4. Remove from the oven, drizzle with the oil, season generously with salt and pepper and toss to coat. Return to the oven for 25–30 minutes, stirring halfway, until golden and crisp.
5. While still hot, drizzle over the vinegar, toss again and let them cool fully on the baking sheet – they'll crisp up a little more as they cool.

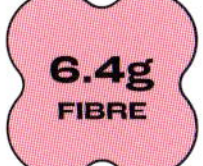

Future you:

Cool and place in an airtight container, storing in the fridge for up to 3 days.
If they soften, re-crisp in a hot oven for 5–10 minutes.

Serves 6 | Prep 5 minutes | Cook 20 minutes

Feta + Olive Egg Cups

GF

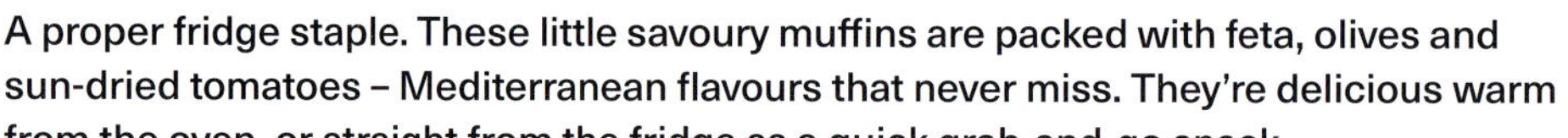

A proper fridge staple. These little savoury muffins are packed with feta, olives and sun-dried tomatoes – Mediterranean flavours that never miss. They're delicious warm from the oven, or straight from the fridge as a quick grab-and-go snack.

6-hole muffin tray, greased or lined with muffin cases

- 4 large/US extra-large eggs
- 50 g/1¾ oz/scant ¼ cup cottage cheese
- 20 g/¾ oz sun-dried tomatoes, finely chopped
- 20 g/¾ oz/scant ¼ cup Kalamata olives, finely chopped
- 20 g/¾ oz spinach, finely chopped
- 30 g/1 oz feta, crumbled
- ¼ tsp black pepper
- ½ tsp dried oregano
- ¼ tsp garlic granules

1. Preheat the oven to 180°C fan/200°C/400°F/gas mark 6.
2. In a large jug or bowl, beat together the eggs and cottage cheese very well until they are smooth and airy. Stir in the chopped sun-dried tomatoes, olives, spinach, feta, pepper, oregano and garlic granules.
3. Divide the mixture evenly among the muffin holes, filling each about three-quarters full.
4. Bake for 18–20 minutes until puffed and golden around the edges.
5. Cool slightly before removing from the muffin tray – they'll firm up as they cool.

Future you:

- Cool and place in an airtight container, storing in the fridge for up to 4 days.
- Cool and freeze for up to 2 months.
- Thaw in the fridge overnight.
- Enjoy cold, or reheat in the microwave for 30 seconds.

Nuggets + BBQ Sauce

I know for a fact that everyone loves nuggets. And just because you're eating a little more healthy-ish doesn't mean you can't have them. These hit every craving and are great hot from the oven or cold from the fridge... if they make it that far.

baking sheet, lined (if using an oven)

- 50 g/1¾ oz/generous 1 cup panko breadcrumbs (GF: gluten-free breadcrumbs)
- ¼ tsp garlic granules
- ¼ tsp onion granules
- ½ tsp smoked paprika
- ¼ tsp dried oregano
- 2 tbsp wholemeal/whole wheat flour (GF: gluten-free flour)
- 1 large/US extra-large egg, beaten
- 2 chicken breasts, cut into bite-sized pieces
- salt and pepper
- olive oil, for cooking

For the BBQ sauce

- 3 tbsp tomato purée/paste
- 1 tbsp maple syrup
- 1 tsp smoked paprika
- ½ tsp crushed chilli flakes/chile flakes
- ¼ tsp garlic granules
- 2 tsp balsamic vinegar

1. Preheat the oven or air fryer to 200°C fan/220°C/425°F/gas mark 7.
2. Heat a drizzle of oil in a non-stick pan over medium heat. Add the panko and toast for 1–2 minutes, stirring often, until lightly golden. Transfer to a shallow bowl and mix in the garlic granules, onion granules, smoked paprika, dried oregano and a good pinch of salt and pepper.
3. Place the flour in one bowl, the beaten egg in another and the seasoned panko in a third.
4. Coat each piece of chicken first in the flour, then in the egg, then in the panko until fully coated.
5. Arrange the nuggets in a single layer on the lined baking sheet or in the air-fryer basket – don't overcrowd them.
6. Bake or air-fry for 12–14 minutes, turning halfway, until golden and cooked through (internal temperature should read 75°C/167°F).
7. While the nuggets cook, whisk all the BBQ sauce ingredients together in a small bowl or jar, adding 1–2 tablespoons of water to loosen, if needed, and seasoning to taste.
8. Serve the nuggets hot with the BBQ sauce for dipping.

Future you:

- Cool and place in an airtight container, storing in the fridge for up to 3 days.
- Cool and freeze the nuggets and sauce separately for up to 2 months.
- Thaw in the fridge overnight.
- Bake or air-fry the nuggets at 180°C fan/200°C/400°F/gas mark 6 for 6–8 minutes until hot and crisp again.

Protein-Packed Platters

I love cooking for others.

There's something really special about everyone digging into one shared platter in the middle of the table. It's generous, unfussy and instantly social – and easily one of my best low-effort hosting hacks. The format is always the same: a bold sauce swooshed straight onto the dish, protein layered on top, then something crunchy and fresh for texture. It looks dramatic, tastes unbelievable and requires far less effort than perfectly plating individual servings. Work smart, not hard. Always.

Serves 3-4 | Prep 20 minutes | Cook 50 minutes

Za'atar Chicken With Olive Rice + Garlicky Yogurt

A spatchcocked chicken always feels like a showstopper, but this one's surprisingly low effort for the reward. Roasted over onions with a zesty za'atar marinade, the tray juices turn to liquid gold – perfect for spooning over the olive-studded rice, which bakes gently in the oven at the same time.

23 x 33-cm/9 x 13-in roasting tray
23 x 15-cm/9 x 6-in baking dish

- 2 onions, cut into thick wedges
- 1 large garlic bulb
- 1 whole chicken (about 1.4–1.6 kg/3–3½ lb), spatchcocked
- grated zest and juice of 2 lemons
- 1 tbsp za'atar
- 1 tsp ground cumin
- 2 tbsp olive oil
- 300 g/10½ oz/1½ cups easy-cook basmati rice
- 450 ml/16 fl oz/scant 2 cups hot chicken stock
- 100 g/3½ oz/1 cup pitted green olives, roughly chopped
- 350 g/12 oz/1½ cups 5% fat Greek yogurt (DF: soy yogurt)
- 1 tbsp finely chopped fresh parsley
- 40 g/1½ oz feta, crumbled (DF: dairy-free cheese)
- salt and pepper
- salad leaves, lightly dressed, to serve

1 Preheat the oven to 220°C fan/240°C/475°F/gas mark 9.

2 Place the onion wedges into the roasting tray. Halve the garlic bulb crossways, drizzle with oil, then wrap tightly in foil and tuck it into a corner of the tray. Place the chicken in the centre, breast-side up.

3 In a small bowl, mix the lemon zest and juice with the za'atar, cumin and olive oil, and generously season. Rub the marinade all over the chicken, letting the excess drip, coating the onions. Roast on the top shelf of the oven for 45–50 minutes, until the chicken is golden and cooked through.

4 Meanwhile, add the rice, hot chicken stock and olives to the smaller baking dish. Stir, cover tightly with foil and place on the lower oven shelf for the final 15 minutes of the chicken's cooking time. Once done, leave the foil on for 2 minutes, then uncover and fluff with a fork.

5 When the chicken is cooked, transfer it to a board and rest for 10 minutes. Reserve the roasting juices.

6 Carefully unwrap the garlic and squeeze the cloves into a bowl. Mash with a fork, then stir in the yogurt with a pinch of seasoning.

7 To finish the rice, stir through the roasted onions, chopped parsley and a tablespoon or two of the chicken's roasting juices.

8 Serve together on a large platter; smear the garlicky yogurt over the base, then pile on the olive rice. Arrange the chicken on top (I like to serve it whole, then carve at the table), and finish with the crumbled feta and a handful of salad leaves on the side.

Future you:

Cool and place in an airtight container, storing in the fridge for up to 3 days.
The chicken can be frozen for up to 2 months. Rice and yoghurt are best fresh.
Thaw in the fridge overnight.
Reheat: Reheat chicken and rice in the microwave until piping hot. Yoghurt should be served cold.

Serves 4–5 | Prep 25 minutes | Cook 25 minutes

Chicken Skewers with Bulgur + Whipped Tahini

DF/O

Technically, this one's two platters, but they're a package deal. When it all comes together, it's everything I love about sharing-style eating. Big flavours, loads of texture, and something gorgeous to stick in the middle of the table.

wooden skewers, soaked for 15 minutes

- 120 g/4 oz/generous ½ cup thick 0–5% fat yogurt (DF/VE: soy yogurt)
- juice of ½ lemon
- 1 tsp garlic powder
- 1 tsp onion powder
- 1 tsp paprika
- 1 tsp dried oregano
- ½ tsp sumac
- 650 g/1 lb 7 oz chicken breast, cut into 2-cm/¾-in chunks (VE: torn smoked tofu)
- salt and pepper
- olive oil, for cooking

For the bulgur

- 200 g/7 oz/scant 1¼ cups bulgur wheat (GF: quinoa)
- 1 x 400-g/14-oz can chickpeas/garbanzo beans, drained and rinsed
- grated zest and juice of 1 lemon
- ½ red onion, finely diced
- 2 tbsp roughly chopped fresh parsley, plus extra to serve

For the cabbage

- 2 sweetheart (hispi) cabbages, quartered lengthways/lengthwise
- 2 tbsp honey (VE: maple syrup)
- 1 tbsp crispy chilli oil/crispy chile oil
- 1 tsp sesame seeds

For the whipped tahini

- 80 g/2¾ oz/¼ cup tahini
- 250 g/9 oz/generous 1 cup thick 0–5% fat yogurt (DF/VE: soy yogurt)
- ½ tsp garlic powder
- juice of ½ lemon
- 1 tsp sesame oil

1. Preheat the oven's grill to 200°C fan/220°C/425°F/gas mark 7.
2. In a bowl, combine the yogurt, lemon juice, spices and a good pinch of seasoning. Add the chicken and toss to coat. Set aside to marinate while you prep everything else (or refrigerate for up to 24 hours).
3. Cook the bulgur according to packet instructions. Drain, if needed, then stir in the chickpeas, lemon zest and juice, red onion, a drizzle of olive oil, parsley and a pinch of salt and pepper.
4. Heat a large frying pan/skillet over medium–high heat. Drizzle the cabbage quarters with olive oil and season, then sear in batches for 2–3 minutes on each cut side until lightly charred.
5. Transfer the cabbage to a baking sheet and place on the bottom shelf of the oven to finish cooking for 20 minutes, or until tender.
6. Meanwhile, thread the chicken onto soaked wooden skewers and place on a baking sheet. Cook directly under the hot grill for 12–14 minutes, turning halfway, until golden and cooked.
7. In a large mixing bowl, whisk together the tahini, yogurt, garlic, lemon juice and sesame oil. Gradually whisk in 2–3 tablespoons of cold water until it's spoonable, then season with salt. Spread the mix over a large platter.
8. Combine the honey and chilli oil in a small bowl and warm briefly (about 10 seconds) to loosen.
9. Arrange the charred cabbage over the whipped tahini, then drizzle with the hot honey and scatter with sesame seeds. Serve the bulgur on a second platter with the chicken skewers and some extra parsley.

Serves 4 | Prep 20 minutes | Cook 25 minutes

Lemon Herb Chicken With Crispy Tomato Rice + Harissa Yogurt

2 large baking sheets, lined

- 600 g/1 lb 7 oz boneless, skinless chicken thighs
- grated zest and juice of 1 lemon
- 2 garlic cloves, grated
- 1 tbsp olive oil
- 1 tsp dried oregano
- ½ tsp ground cumin
- 1 lemon, thinly sliced into rounds
- salt and pepper
- olive oil, for cooking and drizzling

For the rice

- 2 x 250-g/9-oz pouches cooked jasmine rice
- 100 g/3½ oz sun-dried tomatoes in oil, finely chopped, plus 2 tbsp oil from the jar
- 1 garlic clove, finely chopped
- 1 tsp smoked paprika
- ½ tsp chilli flakes/chile flakes (optional)

For the harissa yogurt

- 300 g/10½ oz/1⅓ cups thick 0–5% fat yogurt (DF: soy yogurt)
- 1 tbsp rose or regular harissa paste
- 1 tsp lemon juice

For the herby feta

- 100 g/3½ oz feta, crumbled (DF: vegan feta or omit)
- 2 tbsp finely chopped fresh herbs (parsley, mint or dill)

You'll just have to make this one to understand the texture magic going on. Jasmine rice might not be the obvious pick for a Mediterranean line up, but nothing else gives the same mix of crispy edges and chewy middle when baked. And when you get a bite of everything together, it's pretty special.

1 Preheat the oven to 200°C fan/220°C/425°F/gas mark 7.

2 In a bowl, mix the chicken thighs with the lemon zest and juice, garlic, olive oil, oregano, cumin and a good pinch of salt and pepper. Set aside to marinate while you prepare the rice.

3 Heat the rice pouches in the microwave for 2 minutes. Tip into a bowl and fluff with a fork. Stir through the sun-dried tomatoes and oil from the jar, garlic, smoked paprika, chilli flakes (if using) and a pinch of salt.

4 Spread the rice across one lined baking sheet in a thin layer and bake for 25 minutes until crisped around the edges and golden.

5 Arrange the chicken thighs on the second baking sheet and nestle in the lemon slices. Roast for 25 minutes until the chicken is golden and cooked through and the lemons are caramelized at the edges.

6 While everything cooks, mix the yogurt with harissa, lemon juice and a pinch of salt. In a separate bowl, toss the feta with the herbs and a drizzle of olive oil.

7 To serve, spoon the harissa yogurt across a large platter, then layer over the crispy rice, chicken and roasted lemon rounds. Finish with the herby feta and a final drizzle of olive oil.

Future you:

- Cool and place in an airtight container, storing in the fridge for up to 3 days.
- Cool and freeze the chicken and rice for up to 2 months.
- Thaw in the fridge overnight.
- Reheat in a hot oven for 8–10 minutes, or the microwave for 2–3 minutes, until piping hot.

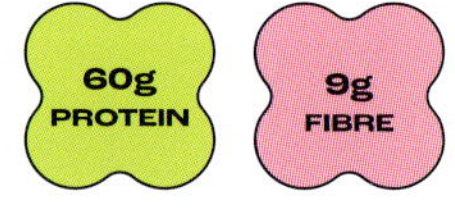

Serves 4 | Prep 20 minutes | Cook 25 minutes

Herb-Crusted Salmon With Mustardy Potatoes, Tzatziki + Crispy Capers

If you're looking for a stress-free hosting recipe, this is it. It looks fancy, tastes incredible and, most importantly, works warm, cold or somewhere in between. You can prep most of it ahead of time and just add the salmon fresh when everyone's at the table.

baking sheet, lined

- grated zest of 1 lemon
- 2 tbsp chopped fresh dill
- 2 tbsp chopped fresh parsley
- 1 garlic clove, grated
- 1 tbsp Dijon mustard
- 1 tbsp olive oil, plus extra for cooking
- 4 salmon fillets
- 2 tbsp capers
- a handful of pea shoots or rocket
- salt and pepper

For the potatoes

- 750 g/1 lb 10 oz baby potatoes
- 1 tbsp wholegrain mustard
- 1 tsp honey
- 1 tbsp finely chopped fresh chives

For the tzatziki

- ½ cucumber, grated and squeezed of excess water
- 300 g/10½ oz thick 0–5% fat yogurt (DF: soy yogurt)
- 1 garlic clove, grated
- 1 tbsp chopped dill
- 1 tsp dried mint (optional)
- grated zest of ½ lemon
- ½ tbsp extra virgin olive oil

1. Preheat the oven to 200°C fan/220°C/425°F/gas mark 7.
2. In a small bowl, mix the lemon zest, dill, parsley, garlic, Dijon mustard, olive oil and a good pinch of salt and pepper to make a thick paste.
3. Place the salmon fillets skin-side down on the baking sheet and spread the herby crust on top. Roast for 10–12 minutes, until just cooked through.
4. While the salmon cooks, halve any larger potatoes, then boil in salted water for 12–15 minutes until knife-tender. Drain and let them steam-dry in the colander.
5. Meanwhile, make the tzatziki by combining all the ingredients with lemon zest, olive oil and a pinch of salt. Stir well and chill until ready to serve.
6. Heat 2 tablespoons of olive oil in a large frying pan/skillet over medium–high heat, then add the potatoes. Cook for 5–7 minutes, crushing some with the back of a spatula, until golden and crisp. Turn off the heat and toss through the wholegrain mustard, honey, chives and a pinch of salt and pepper.
7. In a separate small frying pan, heat a glug of oil over medium heat. Once hot, fry the capers for 1–2 minutes, then drain on kitchen paper.
8. To serve, spread a generous layer of tzatziki across a large platter. Spoon the mustardy potatoes on top. Gently flake apart the salmon fillets and add to the platter with the crispy capers and pea shoots.

Future you:

Cool and place in an airtight container, storing in the fridge for up to 3 days.
Best served fresh, but you can reheat the salmon and potatoes gently in a hot oven, pan or microwave.

Serves 2–3 | Prep 15 minutes | Cook 15 minutes

Harissa Tofu + Hummus

V
VE/O
DF/O
GF/O

If you've got veggie or vegan friends coming round, or just fancy a meat-free spread, this one's an absolute crowd-pleaser. The tofu's sticky and spicy, the hummus silky and rich, and every topping adds freshness or crunch. It looks like effort but really isn't, which is exactly the point.

baking sheet, lined

- ½ red onion, thinly sliced
- juice of ½ lemon
- 1 x 300-g/10½-oz block extra-firm tofu, pressed
- 1 tbsp cornflour/cornstarch
- 1½ tbsp rose harissa paste
- 1 tbsp maple syrup
- 1 tbsp soy sauce (GF: tamari)
- 1 tbsp pomegranate seeds
- 1 tbsp chopped fresh mint
- 1 tbsp chopped fresh parsley
- 40 g/1½ oz feta, crumbled (DF/VE: vegan feta or omit)
- salt and pepper
- olive oil, for cooking
- flatbreads, to serve (GF: gluten-free flatbreads)

For the hummus

- 1 × 400-g/14-oz can chickpeas/garbanzo beans, drained
- 2 heaped tbsp tahini
- juice of 1 lemon
- 1 garlic clove, crushed
- 50 ml/1¾ fl oz/3½ tbsp extra virgin olive oil
- 1–2 ice cubes

1. Preheat the oven to 200°C fan/220°C/425°F/gas mark 7.
2. For the hummus, add the chickpeas, tahini, lemon juice, garlic, olive oil, 1 teaspoon of salt and 1 ice cube to a food processor. Blitz until smooth, stopping to scrape down the sides once or twice. If it's still thick, add the second ice cube and blend again until creamy and fluffy. Adjust the seasoning to taste and set aside.
3. In a small bowl or jar, toss the red onion with the lemon juice and a pinch of salt. Set aside to lightly pickle.
4. Grate the tofu on the coarse side of a cheese grater. Transfer to the lined baking sheet, drizzle lightly with olive oil, season with salt and pepper and toss with the cornflour. Spread into an even layer and bake for 12–15 minutes, until golden and crisp.
5. Whisk together the harissa, maple syrup and soy sauce in a large bowl. Add the baked tofu while still warm and toss until sticky and well coated.
6. Pop the flatbreads into the oven for a few minutes to warm through.
7. Spread the hummus over one side of a large platter. Pile on the harissa tofu, then scatter over the pickled onion, pomegranate, mint, parsley and feta. Tear the flatbreads and nestle to the side for scooping.

Future you:

Cool and place in an airtight container, storing in the fridge for up to 4 days.

Plant Powered

We all know we should be eating more plants.

The good news is that plant-powered meals generally have a built-in advantage: the fibre takes care of itself. Plus, getting more protein from plants naturally brings variety (and keeps your gut very happy). So this time, I wanted to give vegetarian and vegan recipes their own chapter. And although I do eat meat, these are actually my favourite recipes to develop. When you can't rely on meat to do the heavy lifting, you push flavour harder and end up creating something really exciting. Once you make your way through these, I think you'll agree.

Serves 4 | Prep 10 minutes | Cook 25 minutes

Egg Curry

V

DF

GF/O

I had my first egg curry while travelling in India and it's had a spot in my weekly rotation ever since. It's just so comforting and full of flavour, with the hard-boiled eggs beautifully soaking in that spiced sauce. Lucky for us, it's also a brilliant high-protein choice for meat-free nights. I like it with both bread and rice – one for scooping, one for soaking.

- 1 tsp mustard seeds
- 1 tsp fennel seeds
- 1 onion, finely diced
- 1 green chilli/chile, finely diced
- 2.5-cm/1-in piece fresh ginger, grated
- 2 garlic cloves, minced
- 3 large tomatoes, diced
- 2 tsp ground coriander
- 1 tsp ground turmeric
- 3 heaped tbsp tomato purée/paste
- 8 eggs
- 2 tbsp garam masala
- 1 tbsp roughly chopped coriander/cilantro
- 2 x 250-g/9-oz pouches cooked brown basmati rice, or 150 g/5¼ oz rice cooked according to packet instructions
- salt and pepper
- olive or avocado oil, for cooking
- 1 large naan or roti, to serve (GF: gluten-free naan)

1. Heat 1 tablespoon of oil in a large frying pan/skillet over low–medium heat. Add the mustard and fennel seeds and toast for 1–2 minutes until fragrant. They will sputter a little, so use a lid or splash guard for this step.
2. Add the onion and green chilli with a pinch of salt. Cook for about 4 minutes, stirring occasionally, until softened. Stir in the ginger, garlic and tomatoes and cook for 6 minutes more, using a spoon or masher to help break the tomatoes down into a saucy base.
3. Tip in the ground coriander, turmeric, a good pinch of salt and pepper, tomato purée and 300ml/1¼ cups of water. Stir well, bring to a simmer, then reduce the heat to low. Cover and let the curry bubble gently while you prepare the eggs.
4. Bring a large saucepan of water to the boil. Lower in the eggs and cook for 8 minutes. Drain, run under cold water to cool quickly, then peel.
5. Microwave the rice according to the packet instructions.
6. Stir the garam masala into the curry, then add the peeled eggs and let them warm through in the sauce.
7. Top the curry by scattering over fresh coriander. Serve with the rice and bread.

3.7g
FIBRE

Future you:

- Cool and place the curry and rice in separate airtight containers, storing in the fridge for up to 3 days.
- Freeze the curry base for up to 2 months. Boil fresh eggs to serve.
- Thaw in the fridge overnight, or in the microwave on low power.
- Reheat the curry gently in a pan or microwave until piping hot. Add fresh or reheated eggs before serving.

Serves 2 | Prep 10 minutes | Cook 30 minutes

Sticky Chipotle Tofu Loaded Fries

V
VE/O
DF/O
GF

Turning a plate of chips into a main meal? Sign meee up. This is my slightly healthier take, of course – the chips go perfectly crisp in the oven or air fryer (no deep-frying needed), then get piled high with chipotle tofu, Greek yogurt for extra protein and tangy pickled onions for zing. Ten out of ten.

baking sheet, lined (if using an oven)

- 500 g/1 lb 2 oz potatoes
- 1 x 300-g/10½-oz block extra-firm smoked tofu
- 1 tsp cornflour/cornstarch
- 1–2 tbsp chipotle paste, to taste
- 1 tsp maple syrup
- 25 g/1 oz/generous ¼ cup grated cheddar cheese (DF/VE: dairy-free cheese)
- 3 tbsp fat-free Greek yogurt (DF/VE: soy yogurt)
- salt and pepper
- olive oil, for cooking
- coriander/cilantro leaves, to serve

For the quick-pickled onion

- ½ small red onion, thinly sliced
- 2 tbsp white or apple cider vinegar

1. Preheat the air fryer or oven to 220°C fan/240°C/475°F/gas mark 9.

2. Cut the potatoes into thin batons and toss with 1 tablespoon of olive oil and a good pinch of salt and pepper. If using the air fryer: place in the air-fryer basket and cook for 30 minutes. If using the oven: place on the lined baking sheet and roast for 35 minutes, turning halfway, until golden and crisp. Sprinkle over the cheese for the final 2 minutes so it melts over the top.

3. While the chips cook, press any excess water from the tofu, then crumble it into a bowl. Toss with the cornflour and a pinch of salt and pepper. If using the oven: spread the tofu on the prepared baking sheet, drizzle with olive oil and bake for 20 minutes. If using the air fryer: add the tofu to the basket, drizzle with olive oil and cook for 15 minutes until golden and crisp.

4. Meanwhile, make the quick-pickled onion. Combine the red onion with the vinegar and a pinch of salt in a small bowl or jar. Scrunch it together with your fingers to help it soften, then set aside to lightly pickle – it will be ready by the time you serve.

5. Once the tofu is ready, toss it with the chipotle paste and maple syrup until coated and glossy.

6. Pile the cheesy fries onto a platter or tray, then top with the tofu, dollops of yogurt, pickled onion and coriander.

Future you:

- Cool and place in an airtight container, storing in the fridge for up to 2 days.
- The tofu can be frozen after cooking for up to 2 months.
- Thaw in the fridge overnight before reheating. The fries are best fresh.
- Reheat in the oven or air fryer until hot and crisp.

Serves 2 | Prep 15 minutes | Cook 20 minutes

Chilled Soba Noodle Soup + Crispy Tofu

V
VE/O
DF

When it's too warm to even look at the oven, try this – chilled noodles in a cold, creamy, herby coconut soup, topped with crispy tofu. Light but filling and endlessly slurpable. You can mix and match toppings and noodles, but the crispy tofu is non-negotiable.

baking sheet, lined (if using an oven)

- 1 x 280-g/10-oz block extra-firm tofu
- 2 tsp soy sauce (GF: tamari)
- 1 tsp cornflour/cornstarch
- 120 g/4 oz buckwheat soba noodles
- salt and pepper
- olive oil, for cooking

For the soup base

- 2.5-cm/1-in piece fresh ginger, peeled
- 2 garlic cloves
- 1 tbsp peanut butter
- ½ tsp white miso paste (GF: check label)
- 400 ml/14 fl oz/1¾ cups light coconut milk
- 2 tsp honey (VE: maple syrup)
- 2 tsp soy sauce (GF: tamari)
- 2 tsp rice vinegar
- 15 g/½ oz fresh coriander/cilantro (about ½ bunch), plus extra to serve
- 10 g/⅓ oz fresh basil (about ⅓ bunch), plus extra to serve
- 2 ice cubes

To serve

- ¼ cucumber, thinly sliced
- 1 small red chilli/chile, thinly sliced
- 1 tsp sesame seeds

30.4g PROTEIN

6.2g FIBRE

1 Preheat the air fryer or oven to 200°C fan/220°C/425°F/gas mark 7.

2 Press out any water from the block of tofu (this will vary depending on the brand you use), then tear it into small chunks. Transfer the pieces to a large mixing bowl or lidded container along with the soy sauce, cornflour and a good pinch of salt and pepper. Mix well until each chunk is coated.

3 If using an oven: spread out the tofu evenly on the lined baking sheet. Drizzle with a little oil and bake for 20 minutes. If using an air fryer: add the tofu to the air-fryer basket, drizzle with oil and cook for 10–12 minutes until golden and crisp.

4 While the tofu cooks, bring a pan of water to the boil and cook the soba noodles according to the packet instructions. Drain, rinse under cold water and set aside to chill.

5 While the noodles cook, make the soup base. Place the ginger, garlic, peanut butter, miso, coconut milk, honey, soy sauce, rice vinegar, herbs and ice cubes into a blender. Blitz until completely smooth, then transfer to the fridge to chill.

6 Divide the chilled noodles between two bowls and pour over the cold soup base. Top with the crispy tofu, cucumber, chilli, sesame seeds and extra herbs.

Future you:

- Cool and place in an airtight container, storing in the fridge for up to 3 days.
- The soup base can be frozen for up to 1 month.
- Thaw in the fridge overnight, or in the microwave on low power. Re-blend or whisk before serving.
- The soup is served cold. The tofu can be reheated in a pan or air fryer, if preferred hot.

OPINEL
SAVOIE · FRANCE

Serves 4 | Prep 25 minutes | Cook 30 minutes

Meatless Balls Al Forno

V
VE/O
DF/O
GF/O

I tested a lot of meat-free meatballs before landing on these, and most were either dry, crumbly or forgettable. These are none of those things. They're about as high in plant-based protein as you can get, they have a satisfying bite, and the leftovers are phenomenal in a sub roll the next day... if you have any left.

- 200-g/7-oz block tempeh
- 1 x 400-g/14-oz can green lentils, drained and rinsed
- ½ tsp onion granules
- ½ tsp garlic granules
- 1 tsp dried oregano
- 3 sun-dried tomatoes, chopped
- 15 g/½ oz/3 tbsp grated vegetarian Parmesan (DF/VE: nutritional yeast)
- 1 egg (VE: mix 1 tbsp ground flaxseed/linseed with 2½ tbsp water, and leave to rest for 5 minutes)
- 30 g/1 oz/⅔ cup panko breadcrumbs (GF: gluten-free breadcrumbs)
- 1 light mozzarella ball (DF/VE: 50 g/1¾ oz dairy-free cheese)
- salt and pepper
- olive oil, for cooking

For the tomato sauce

- 1 red onion, finely chopped
- 2 garlic cloves, minced
- ½ tsp dried oregano
- 2 x 400-g/14-oz cans plum tomatoes
- 1 tbsp balsamic vinegar

For the garlic bread

- 4 slices sourdough (GF: gluten-free bread)
- 1½ tbsp extra virgin olive oil
- 1 small garlic clove

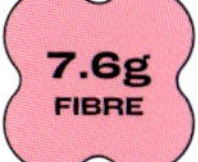

1. Preheat the oven to 200°C fan/220°C/425°F/gas mark 7.
2. Crumble the tempeh into a food processor. Add the lentils, onion granules, garlic granules, oregano, sun-dried tomatoes, cheese, egg, breadcrumbs and a good pinch of salt and pepper. Pulse to a thick, textured paste – you still want some bite, so avoid over-blending.
3. With damp hands, form the mixture into 16 small balls. Place on the lined baking sheet, drizzle generously with olive oil and bake for 8 minutes. Flip them over, then bake for another 8 minutes until golden and firm.
4. Meanwhile, make the sauce. Heat 1 tablespoon of oil in a large ovenproof frying pan/skillet over medium heat. Cook the onion for about 4 minutes until softened, then add the garlic and oregano and cook for 1 minute more.
5. Tip in the plum tomatoes, breaking them up with a spoon. Add the balsamic vinegar and a pinch of salt and pepper. Simmer gently for 15 minutes, stirring occasionally.
6. Preheat the grill/broiler to high.
7. Nestle the baked meatballs into the sauce and turn to coat. Tear over the mozzarella and place the pan under the grill for 3–5 minutes until the cheese is melted and bubbling.
8. For the garlic bread, drizzle the sourdough with olive oil and toast in a hot pan or under the grill until golden on both sides. Rub one side with the cut garlic, then serve alongside the meatballs.

Future you:

- Cool and place in an airtight container, storing in the fridge for up to 3 days.
- Cool and freeze the meatballs and sauce for up to 2 months. The garlic bread is best fresh.
- Thaw in the fridge overnight.
- Reheat gently in a pan or microwave until piping hot.

Serves 2 | Prep 15 minutes | Cook 15–20 minutes

Tofu Doner

V

VE/O

DF/O

GF/O

Some nights call for a bit of comfort, and this take on a doner kebab hits all the right spots – albeit in a more healthy-ish way. The thin, crisped ribbons give you that chewy, meaty texture, while the fresh salad and garlicky yogurt sauce pull it all together. Proof that the best fakeaway nights can absolutely be plant-powered.

baking sheet, lined

- ½ red onion, finely diced
- 2 salad tomatoes, finely diced
- ¼ small cucumber, finely diced
- 1 tbsp finely chopped fresh parsley
- 1 tbsp finely chopped fresh mint
- 2 flatbreads (GF: gluten-free flatbreads)
- salt and pepper
- lemon wedges, to serve

For the doner 'meat'

- 2 tbsp olive oil
- 2 tbsp tomato purée/paste
- juice of 1 lemon
- 1 garlic clove, minced
- 1 tsp ground cumin
- 1 tsp smoked paprika
- 1 tsp onion granules
- ½ tsp cayenne pepper
- 225 g/8 oz extra-firm smoked tofu, pressed

For the garlic sauce

- 100 g/3½ oz/scant ½ cup thick 0–5% fat yogurt (DF/VE: soy yogurt)
- 1 garlic clove, minced
- juice of ½ lemon

1 Preheat the oven to 220°C fan/240°C/475°F/gas mark 9.

2 To make the doner 'meat', whisk together the olive oil, tomato purée, lemon juice, garlic, cumin, smoked paprika, onion granules and cayenne pepper in a large bowl. Season generously with salt and pepper. Using a potato peeler or mandoline, shave the tofu into thin ribbons. Add to the bowl and toss gently to coat.

3 Spread the seasoned tofu out on the lined baking sheet and bake for 15–20 minutes, or until slightly crisp and curling at the edges.

4 Meanwhile, combine the red onion, tomatoes, cucumber, parsley and mint in a bowl. Season with salt and pepper and set aside.

5 For the garlic sauce, stir together the yogurt, garlic and lemon juice in a small bowl. Season to taste.

6 To assemble, warm your flatbreads (optional, but recommended). Spread with garlic sauce, then layer on the salad and the crispy tofu 'doner'. Drizzle with more sauce and add a wedge of lemon on the side, if you like.

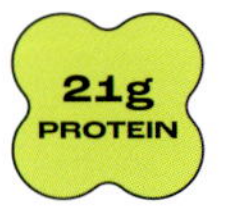

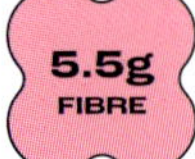

Future you:

Cool and place in an airtight container, storing in the fridge for up to 3 days.
Cool and freeze the cooked tofu for up to 2 months.
Thaw in the fridge overnight.
Reheat the tofu in a frying pan/skillet or microwave until warmed through. Assemble the rest fresh.

Serves 2 | Prep 15 minutes | Cook 20 minutes

Pineapple Lime Skewers + Herby Rice

GF/O

There's something about this combo that just screams sunshine. Sweet, sticky tofu with that sharp hit of lime and plenty of fresh herbs – it's fresh, bright and a proper mood-booster. Bonus points for how easy it is, too.

wooden skewers, soaked for 15 minutes

- 225 g/8 oz extra-firm tofu, pressed and cut into cubes
- 1 red onion, cut into wedges
- 200-g/7-oz can pineapple chunks in juice
- 1 courgette/zucchini, cut into half moons
- 1 tbsp sesame oil
- salt and pepper

For the glaze

- 80 ml/2¾ fl oz/⅓ cup pineapple juice (from the pineapple can)
- juice of 1½ limes
- 2 tbsp soy sauce (GF: tamari)
- 1 garlic clove, minced
- 2.5-cm/1-in piece fresh ginger, peeled and grated
- ½ tsp chilli flakes/chile flakes
- 1 tbsp maple syrup
- 1 tsp cornflour/cornstarch

For the herby rice

- 1 x 250-g/9-oz pouch cooked rice
- ½ tbsp finely chopped fresh parsley
- ½ tbsp finely chopped fresh coriander/cilantro
- juice of ½ lime

1. Preheat the oven to 200°C fan/220°C/425°F/gas mark 7 on the oven grill/broiler setting.
2. Start by making the glaze. In a small bowl or jar, combine the pineapple juice, lime juice, soy sauce, garlic, ginger, chilli flakes, maple syrup, cornflour and 2 tablespoons of water. Whisk or shake to combine. Pour into a small frying pan/skillet set over medium heat and cook for 2–3 minutes, stirring often, until thickened and glossy. Remove from the heat and set aside.
3. Next, prepare your skewers. Thread the tofu cubes, red onion, pineapple and courgette onto the soaked skewers, alternating as you go. Arrange on the lined baking sheet, brush lightly with sesame oil and season with salt and pepper.
4. Place the skewers under the grill and cook for 10–12 minutes, turning every few minutes for even colour. In the final few minutes, brush generously with the glaze on both sides (reserving 2 tablespoons for drizzling at the end), then return to the grill until sticky and caramelized.
5. While the skewers cook, microwave the rice according to the packet instructions. Fluff with a fork, then stir through the parsley, coriander and lime juice and season to taste.
6. Serve the skewers on top of the herby rice and drizzle with the reserved glaze.

Future you:

- Cool and place in an airtight container, storing in the fridge for up to 3 days.
- Remove from the skewers, cool and freeze the tofu for up to 2 months.
- Thaw in the fridge overnight.
- Enjoy cold, or microwave for 2–3 minutes until hot.

Serves 4 | Prep 15 minutes | Cook 30 minutes

Rich Rigatoni Ragu

V
VE/O
DF/O

N

Rich, hearty and a great source of protein without trying to impersonate meat. The walnuts bring fat and body, the lentils give protein and texture, and the sauce develops that slow-cooked depth in very little time. Proper comfort food that still feels weeknight friendly.

- 1 onion, roughly chopped
- 2 carrots, roughly chopped
- 2 sticks/stalks celery, roughly chopped
- 200 g/7 oz chestnut mushrooms
- 4 sun-dried tomatoes
- 150 g/5¼ oz/generous 1 cup walnut halves
- 3 garlic cloves, minced
- 1 × 250-g/9-oz pouch cooked beluga lentils
- 2 tbsp tomato purée/paste
- 150 ml/5 fl oz/⅔ cup red wine (optional)
- 2 × 400-g/14-oz can chopped tomatoes
- 500 ml/18 fl oz/2 cups vegetable stock
- 2 tsp soy sauce (GF: tamari)
- 1 tsp Marmite (optional)
- 2 tsp dried oregano
- 1 tsp dried thyme
- 1 bay leaf
- 250 g/9 oz dried rigatoni (GF: gluten-free pasta)
- salt and pepper
- olive oil, for cooking
- 1 tbsp thinly sliced fresh basil
- vegetarian Parmesan (V) or nutritional yeast (VE/DF), to serve

1. Add the onion, carrots and celery to a food processor with the mushrooms and sun-dried tomatoes. Blitz until finely chopped – you may need to work in batches, depending on the size of your processor. Tip out into a bowl, then add the walnuts and pulse to a coarse crumb.
2. Heat a glug of olive oil in a large pan over medium heat. Add the blitzed veg and cook for 6–8 minutes, stirring often, until softened and starting to caramelize.
3. Stir in the minced garlic, walnuts and lentils, and cook for a couple more minutes until fragrant and the walnuts smell toasty.
4. Mix in the tomato purée and let it cook out for a minute, then pour in the red wine, if using. Allow it to bubble away until reduced by half.
5. Stir through the chopped tomatoes, stock, soy sauce, Marmite (if using), oregano, thyme and bay leaf. Season generously, bring to a simmer, then lower the heat and cook gently for about 20 minutes, stirring occasionally, until thick and glossy. Add a splash more stock if it looks dry.
6. Meanwhile, cook the pasta according to the packet instructions in a large pot of salted boiling water until al dente, then drain.
7. Remove the bay leaf, taste and adjust the seasoning. Stir through the rigatoni until well coated.
8. Finish with the basil and serve with nutritional yeast or vegetarian Parmesan.

29g PROTEIN

14g FIBRE

Future you:

- Cool and place in an airtight container, storing in the fridge for up to 4 days.
- Cool and freeze for up to 3 months.
- Thaw in the fridge overnight.
- Reheat gently on the hob or in the microwave until warmed through, loosening with a splash of water if needed.

Serves 2 | Prep 15 minutes | Cook 20 minutes

Tofu Thai Green Curry

V

DF
GF/O

This is my lazy Thai green curry and I absolutely love it, so I hope you do too. By adding a few extra bits to a storebought curry paste you get something that punches well above its weight. Fragrant, creamy and super satisfying – a perfect weeknight dinner.

- 1 tbsp olive oil
- 1 x 300-g/10½-oz block extra-firm tofu, pressed and cut into cubes
- 1 tbsp cornflour/cornstarch
- 1 tbsp coconut oil
- 3 tbsp Thai green curry paste
- 1 garlic clove, minced
- 1 tsp miso paste
- 1 × 400-ml/14-oz can light coconut milk
- 200 ml/7 fl oz/scant 1 cup vegetable stock
- 1 tbsp light soy sauce (GF: tamari)
- 1 tsp coconut sugar
- 4 kaffir lime leaves
- 1 red (bell) pepper, thinly sliced
- 100 g/3½ oz Tenderstem broccoli, cut into thirds
- 100 g/3½ oz baby corn, cut into chunks
- salt and pepper
- 1 × 250-g/9-oz pouch cooked jasmine rice, to serve
- red chilli, de-seeded and sliced, to serve (optional)

1. Heat the olive oil in a large frying pan/skillet over medium–high heat. Toss the tofu with the cornflour and a pinch of salt and pepper, then fry for 6–8 minutes, turning often, until golden on all sides. Transfer to a plate and set aside.
2. Lower the heat to medium and add the coconut oil to the same pan. Stir in the green curry paste, garlic and miso, and cook for 1 minute until fragrant.
3. Pour in the coconut milk, stock, soy sauce and coconut sugar. Stir to combine, bring to a gentle boil, then reduce to a simmer.
4. Add the lime leaves, red pepper, broccoli and corn. Simmer for 8–10 minutes, or until the vegetables are just tender and the sauce slightly thickened. In the final minute, stir in the tofu to warm through.
5. Meanwhile, microwave the rice according to the packet instructions.
6. Divide the rice between bowls and spoon the curry over the top, adding some extra chilli if you like an extra-spicy kick.

27g PROTEIN

8g FIBRE

Future you:

- Cool and place in an airtight container, storing in the fridge for up to 3 days.
- Cool and freeze the curry (without the rice) for up to 2 months.
- Thaw in the fridge overnight.
- Reheat in the microwave or on the hob until piping hot, adding a splash of water to loosen if needed.

Serves 4 | Prep 10 minutes | Cook 20–25 minutes

Mixed Bean Chilli

V
VE/O
DF/O
GF

Everyone needs a go-to chilli recipe, and this has been mine since long before I stopped eating red meat at home. It's comforting, hearty and so full of flavour, and gets even better with time. Perfect for a bit of accidental meal prep over the next few days.

- 1 onion, finely diced
- 3 garlic cloves, minced
- 4 tbsp tomato purée/paste
- 1 × 700-g/1 lb 9-oz jar or 2 × 400-g/14-oz cans red or black beans
- 1 × 400-g/14-oz can mixed beans, drained and rinsed
- 1 × 400-g/14-oz can chopped tomatoes
- 1 vegetable stock cube
- 200 ml/7 fl oz/scant 1 cup boiling water
- 1 square (10 g/⅓ oz) dark/bittersweet chocolate
- olive oil, for cooking

For the spice mix

- 1 tbsp smoked paprika
- 1–2 tsp chilli powder/chile powder
- 1 tbsp ground cumin
- 2 tsp ground coriander
- 1 tsp dried mixed herbs
- 1 tsp salt
- ¼ tsp black pepper

To serve

- 2 × 250-g/9-oz pouches cooked rice
- thick 0–5% fat yogurt (DF/VE: soy yogurt)
- fresh coriander/cilantro
- lime wedges
- corn tortilla chips (optional)

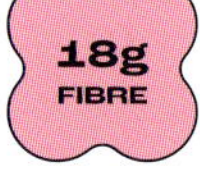

1 Combine all the spice mix ingredients and set aside.

2 Heat a glug of olive oil in a large pan over medium heat. Add the onion and cook for 4–5 minutes until slightly softened. Add the garlic, stir for 1 minute, then add the tomato purée and the spice mix. Cook for 1–2 minutes, stirring often, until fragrant and the purée darkens slightly.

3 Tip in the can of red or black beans with their brine, along with the drained mixed beans, chopped tomatoes and the stock cube. Pour in the boiling water and stir well.

4 Bring to a gentle boil, then reduce the heat and let it simmer for 10–15 minutes, stirring occasionally, until thickened and glossy. With 5 minutes to go, drop in the chocolate and let it melt into the sauce. Taste and adjust the seasoning, adding a splash more water if it looks too thick.

5 Meanwhile, microwave the rice according to packet instructions.

6 Serve the chilli in bowls with rice, a dollop of yoghurt, fresh coriander, lime wedges and a few tortilla chips, if using.

Future you:

- Cool and place in an airtight container, storing in the fridge for up to 4 days.
- Cool and freeze the chilli for up to 3 months.
- Thaw in the fridge overnight.
- Reheat gently on the hob or in the microwave until piping hot, adding a splash of water if needed.

Serves 3 | Prep 10 minutes | Cook 20 minutes

Tuscan Chickpeas + Grains

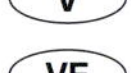

DF
GF/O

Creamy, herby and full of flavour, this to me is plant-based comfort at its best. The silken tofu gives the sauce its velvety texture without cream, while the chickpeas make it properly hearty and an extra source of protein and fibre. One that works just as well in the depths of winter as it does on a summer evening.

- 150 g/5¼ oz silken tofu
- 1 tbsp nutritional yeast
- juice of ½ lemon, plus extra to serve
- 2 tsp Dijon mustard
- 1 onion, finely diced
- 2 garlic cloves, minced
- 60 g/2¼ oz sun-dried tomatoes, plus 1 tbsp of their oil
- 60 g/2¼ oz cherry tomatoes, halved
- 2 tbsp tomato purée/paste
- 1 tsp dried oregano
- 1 tsp smoked paprika
- 1 x 400-g/14-oz can chickpeas/garbanzo beans, drained and rinsed
- 100 g/3½ oz spinach
- 200 g/7 oz Tenderstem broccoli
- ½ tbsp olive oil
- 1 garlic clove, thinly sliced
- ¼ tsp chilli flakes/chile flakes
- 1 x 250-g/9-oz pouch cooked mixed grains (GF: quinoa)
- a handful of basil leaves, sliced
- salt and pepper

1. In a blender (or using a stick blender), whizz together the silken tofu, nutritional yeast, lemon juice and Dijon mustard until smooth. Set aside.
2. Heat the sun-dried tomato oil in a frying pan/skillet over medium heat. Add the onion and cook for 4 minutes until softened, then stir in the sun-dried tomatoes, cherry tomatoes and garlic. Cook for another 4–5 minutes until the tomatoes start to soften and break down slightly.
3. Squash the tomatoes gently with a spoon, then add the tomato purée, oregano and smoked paprika and cook for 1 minute to toast the spices. Add the chickpeas, season well, and cook for 2–3 minutes before pouring in the blended tofu mixture. Stir and cook gently for a few minutes until creamy, then fold in the spinach and cook for another couple of minutes until wilted. Taste and adjust the seasoning, adding extra lemon juice if you like it punchy.
4. Meanwhile, microwave or boil the broccoli until just tender, then drain.
5. Heat the olive oil in a separate frying pan over medium–high heat. Add the broccoli and garlic and fry for 3–4 minutes until the broccoli is lightly charred. Sprinkle over the chilli flakes and a pinch of salt.
6. Microwave the grains according to the packet instructions.
7. Spoon the grains into bowls and top with the creamy chickpeas and garlicky broccoli. Finish off with extra lemon juice and sprinkle over the basil.

Future you:

- Cool and place in an airtight container, storing in the fridge for up to 3 days.
- Cool and freeze the chickpeas for up to 2 months.
- Thaw in the fridge overnight.
- Reheat gently on the hob or in the microwave until hot, adding a splash of water if needed.

Serves 3 | Prep 10 minutes | Cook 25 minutes

Crispy Rice Salad

DF

GF/O

This is not your average rice salad. It's crispy, crunchy and so full of flavour, with a creamy nutty dressing that makes every bite rather addictive. I love it piled up just as it is, or straight from the fridge the next day. I'm hungry just thinking about it.

baking sheet, lined

- 2 x 250-g/9-oz pouches cooked jasmine rice
- 1 tbsp crispy chilli oil/crispy chile oil
- 200 g/7 oz tempeh, cut into small cubes
- 6 small cucumbers (about 200 g/7 oz)
- 1 small head Chinese cabbage
- 1 carrot
- 2 spring onions/scallions
- 10 g/⅓ oz fresh coriander
- 10 g/⅓ oz fresh mint
- 1 red chilli/chile
- 100 g/3½ oz edamame beans
- salt and pepper
- olive oil, for cooking

For the dressing

- 2 tbsp tahini
- 2 tbsp soy sauce (GF: tamari)
- 1 tbsp sesame oil
- 1 garlic clove
- 2.5-cm/1-in piece fresh ginger, peeled and grated
- juice of ½ lime
- 1 tbsp maple syrup

1. Preheat the oven to 200°C fan/220°C/425°F/gas mark 7.

2. Microwave the rice pouches for 1 minute 30 seconds each to loosen them up. Tip out onto the lined baking sheet, drizzle with crispy chilli oil and toss to coat. Spread evenly and bake for 25 minutes, or until golden and crisp around the edges. Let it cool slightly before handling and don't break it up too much – a few crispy clumps are ideal for texture.

3. On a second baking sheet, spread out the tempeh cubes. Drizzle with olive oil, season with salt and pepper and bake for 20 minutes until golden and crisp.

4. While that's going, prep the veg for the salad. Thinly slice the cucumbers (a mandoline makes this quicker), shred the cabbage and carrot, slice the spring onions, finely chop the herbs and chilli, and thaw the edamame, if frozen.

5. Combine the dressing ingredients with 1 tablespoon of water in a jar. Seal and shake until smooth and creamy.

6. Toss the crispy rice and tempeh with the veg, herbs and dressing in a big bowl until well coated. Serve warm, or cold – it's delicious either way.

Future you:

Cool and place in an airtight container, storing in the fridge for up to 3 days.

Serves 2 | Prep 15 minutes | Cook 10 minutes

Gochujang Tofu Bowls

V

DF
GF/O

Sweet, spicy and seriously satisfying. These bowls tick every box: crisp tofu, a punchy glaze and a refreshing cucumber-avocado salad to balance it all out. Just a heads-up, gochujang varies in strength (if yours comes in a tiny jar, it's probably extra-potent), so start with less and add more to taste.

baking sheet, lined

- 1 x 300-g/10½-oz block extra-firm tofu, pressed
- 2 tsp cornflour/cornstarch
- 1 x 250-g/9-oz pouch cooked quinoa
- salt and pepper
- olive oil, for cooking

For the cucumber avocado salad

- juice of 1 lime
- 1 tbsp sesame oil
- 1 tbsp soy sauce (GF: tamari)
- 1 small cucumber, sliced into half-moons
- 1 small avocado, diced
- 2 spring onions/scallions, thinly sliced, plus extra to serve
- 1 tbsp chopped fresh coriander/cilantro
- ½ tsp sesame seeds, plus extra to serve

For the gochujang glaze

- 1–2 tbsp gochujang paste (GF: check label)
- 1 tbsp soy sauce (GF: tamari)
- juice of 1 lime
- 1 tbsp maple syrup
- 2 tsp sesame oil
- 1 garlic clove, minced
- 1 tsp cornflour/cornstarch

28g PROTEIN

10.5g FIBRE

1 Preheat the oven to 200°C fan/220°C/425°F/gas mark 7.

2 Tear the tofu into bite-sized chunks, then toss with the cornflour, a drizzle of oil and a pinch of salt and pepper until evenly coated. Spread out on the tray and bake for 20 minutes, turning once, until golden and crisp.

3 While the tofu cooks, make the cucumber avocado salad. Whisk together the lime juice, sesame oil and soy sauce in a small bowl or jar. Add the cucumber, avocado, spring onions, coriander and sesame seeds. Season to taste with salt and pepper, then toss gently and set aside.

4 Whisk together all the glaze ingredients with 4 tablespoons of water in a small bowl or jar until smooth.

5 Set a small pan over medium heat and pour in the glaze. Cook for 2–3 minutes, stirring often, until thickened and glossy. Add the baked tofu and toss to coat until sticky.

6 Warm the quinoa according to the packet instructions, then divide between bowls. Top with the glazed tofu and a generous spoonful of the cucumber salad. Finish with extra sesame seeds and spring onions to serve.

Future you:

- Cool and place in an airtight container, storing in the fridge for up to 3 days.
- Cool and freeze the tofu and quinoa for up to 2 months. The salad is best fresh.
- Thaw in the fridge overnight.
- Reheat the tofu and quinoa in the microwave until hot. Assemble the salad fresh.

Serves 4 | Prep 10 minutes | Cook 25 minutes

Broccoli Pea-Sto Pasta

V
VE
DF
GF/O
NF/O

When you fancy a big fat bowl of pasta but still want something that feels nourishing, this is how to do it. The homemade pesto blends broccoli, peas and basil with creamy cashews and nutritional yeast for richness, ending up as high in goodness as it is in flavour. A total weeknight win.

baking sheet, lined

- 1 red (bell) pepper, cut into chunks
- 1 yellow (bell) pepper, cut into chunks
- 1 red onion, cut into chunks
- 1 courgette/zucchini, cut into chunks
- 1 x 400-g/14-oz can chickpeas/garbanzo beans, drained
- 2 tsp dried Italian herbs
- 60 g/2¼ oz cherry tomatoes
- 250 g/9 oz dried pasta of choice (GF: gluten-free pasta)
- salt and pepper
- olive oil, for cooking

For the pea-sto

- 200 g/7 oz broccoli
- 100 g/3½ oz/¾ cup frozen petit pois
- 20 g/¾ oz fresh basil
- 2 garlic cloves
- 30 g/1 oz/¼ cup cashews (NF: sunflower seeds)
- 5 tbsp nutritional yeast
- 3 tbsp extra virgin olive oil
- 1 tsp salt
- ¼ tsp pepper

1 Preheat the oven to 210°C fan/230°C/450°F/gas mark 8.

2 Put the peppers, red onion and courgette chunks onto the lined baking sheet along with the chickpeas. Toss with a drizzle of olive oil, the Italian herbs and a good pinch of salt and pepper until coated. Spread out and roast for 20 minutes, adding the cherry tomatoes for the final 10 minutes.

3 Meanwhile, for the pea-sto, add the broccoli and peas to a microwave-safe bowl with a splash of water. Cover and microwave for 3–4 minutes until tender, then drain, run under cold water to cool and drain again. Set aside.

4 Cook the pasta according to the packet instructions in a large pot of salted boiling water until al dente. Scoop out a large mugful of starchy pasta water before draining.

5 Add the broccoli, peas, basil, garlic, cashews, nutritional yeast, olive oil and salt and pepper to a food processor. Blitz until relatively smooth, then pour in about 100 ml/3½ fl oz/6½ tbsp of the pasta water and blend again until creamy.

6 Toss the pasta with the pea-sto until well coated, loosening with another splash of pasta water, if needed. Finally, fold through the roasted veg and chickpeas. Taste and season with salt and pepper if needed, then serve.

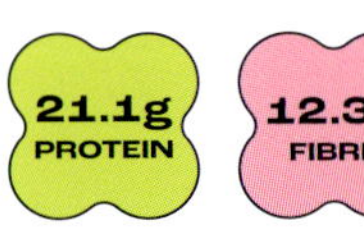

Future you:

- Cool and place in an airtight container, storing in the fridge for up to 4 days.
- Cool and freeze for up to 2 months.
- Thaw in the fridge overnight.
- Enjoy cold or reheat gently in a pan or microwave with a splash of water until warmed through.

Palak Tofu With Homemade Garlic Naan

Inspired by the classic Indian dish palak paneer, this plant-based version swaps cheese for golden tofu and it works a treat. The spinach sauce is creamy, rich and full of spice, and when you scoop it up with homemade garlic naan, it is pure comfort.

- 1 x 300-g/10½-oz block extra-firm tofu, pressed
- 1 tsp cornflour/cornstarch
- ½ large onion, diced
- 1 tsp fennel seeds
- 1 tsp ground coriander
- ½ tsp ground turmeric
- 1 tsp ground cumin
- 1 tsp garam masala
- 2 salad tomatoes, chopped
- 1 green chilli/chile, finely chopped
- 3 garlic cloves, minced
- 2.5-cm/1-in piece fresh ginger, peeled and grated
- 300 g/10½ oz spinach
- 50 ml/1¾ fl oz/3½ tbsp soy cream
- 10 g/⅓ oz fresh coriander/cilantro
- juice of ½ lemon
- salt and pepper
- olive oil, for cooking

For the naans

- 100 g/3½ oz/¾ cup plain/all-purpose flour
- 75 g/2¾ oz/⅓ cup thick fat-free yogurt (DF/VE: soy yogurt), plus extra to serve
- 1 garlic clove, minced
- 2 tsp finely chopped fresh coriander/cilantro
- 1 tbsp olive oil

1 Start by making the naans. In a mixing bowl, combine the flour, yogurt and a pinch of salt to form a rough dough. Knead on a lightly floured surface until smooth, then divide into two oval-shaped portions.

2 Heat a drizzle of olive oil in a non-stick pan over medium heat and cook the naans for 1–2 minutes per side until puffed and golden. Mix together the garlic, coriander and olive oil with a pinch of salt and brush over the naans while they're still warm. Set aside.

3 Cut the tofu into cubes and season, then toss with the cornflour for extra crispiness. Heat a glug of olive oil in a large non-stick pan over medium heat and fry for 6–8 minutes, turning often, until golden. Remove from the pan and set aside.

4 In the same pan, add a touch more oil if needed and sauté the onion for about 8 minutes until softened. Stir in the spices, and cook for 1 minute until fragrant. Add the tomatoes, green chilli, garlic and ginger, and cook for 3–4 minutes until the tomatoes start to break down. Gradually add the spinach, letting it wilt. Remove from the heat.

5 Transfer the curry base to a blender or food processor. Add the soy cream, coriander and a splash of water, then season generously. Blend until smooth and silky.

6 Pour the sauce back into the pan, add the crispy tofu and warm through gently. Finish with a squeeze of lemon juice.

7 Drizzle a little yogurt over the palak tofu, and serve up with the garlic naans for dunking.

Future you:

- Cool and place in an airtight container, storing in the fridge for up to 3 days.
- Cool and freeze the curry and naans separately for up to 2 months.
- Thaw in the fridge overnight.
- Reheat the curry in the microwave or a pan, adding a splash of water to loosen. Recrisp the naan in a hot oven.

Serves 2 | Prep 10 minutes | Cook 25 minutes

Burst Tomato Lentil Bowl

DF
GF/O

There's something so satisfying about a meal that feels both cosy and fresh, and this one nails it. The lentils are rich and smoky, the tofu's crisp and lemony, and it all comes together with a creamy tahini drizzle. A balanced, high-protein dinner that feels way fancier than it is.

baking sheet, lined

- 1 x 300-g/10½-oz block extra-firm tofu, pressed and torn into bite-sized chunks
- 1 heaped tsp cornflour/cornstarch
- grated zest of ½ lemon
- ½ tsp garlic powder
- ½ tsp dried oregano
- 1 onion, finely chopped
- 150 g/5¼ oz cherry tomatoes on the vine
- 2 garlic cloves, thinly sliced
- 1 tsp smoked paprika
- 1 tsp ground cumin
- 2 tbsp tomato purée/paste
- 1 × 250-g/9-oz pouch cooked beluga lentils
- 250 ml/9 fl oz/1 cup vegetable stock
- 1 tsp soy sauce (GF: tamari)
- 150 g/5¼ oz giant couscous
- juice of ½ lemon
- 1 tbsp tahini
- ½ tbsp chopped fresh parsley
- salt and pepper
- olive oil, for cooking

1. Preheat the oven to 200°C fan/220°C/425°F/gas mark 7.
2. Toss the tofu with the cornflour, lemon zest, garlic powder, oregano and a pinch of salt and pepper. Spread out on the lined baking sheet and drizzle with olive oil. Bake for 20 minutes, turning halfway, until golden and crisp.
3. Meanwhile, heat a glug of olive oil in a deep frying pan/skillet over medium heat. Add the onion and cherry tomatoes and cook for 5–6 minutes until the tomatoes start to burst and release their juices. Stir in the garlic, paprika and cumin and cook for another minute, until fragrant. Add the tomato purée, lentils, stock and soy sauce. Bring to the boil, then lower the heat and simmer for 8–10 minutes until thickened and saucy. Season generously.
4. While the lentils cook, prepare the giant couscous according to the packet instructions. Drain, then toss with the lemon juice and a little salt and pepper.
5. Whisk the tahini with 2–3 tablespoons of cold water (add gradually) until smooth and pourable – it may seize at first, but keep whisking and it will loosen.
6. To serve, divide the couscous between bowls. Spoon over the smoky lentils, top with the crispy tofu, drizzle over the tahini and sprinkle over the parsley.

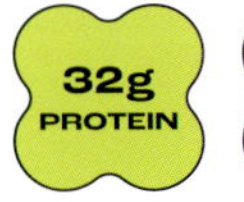

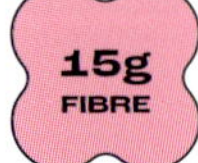

Future you:

- Cool and place in an airtight container, storing in the fridge for up to 3 days.
- Cool and freeze the lentils and tofu separately for up to 2 months.
- Thaw in the fridge overnight.
- Reheat gently in a pan or microwave until piping hot, then reassemble and drizzle with fresh tahini.

Serves 2 | Prep 5 minutes | Cook 10 minutes

Sticky Tempeh Bowl

V

GF/O

Everyone needs a quick, foolproof dinner up their sleeve, and this one's mine. It's sweet, spicy and sticky in all the right ways. And yes, it really does take 15 minutes. So no excuses!

- 1 × 250-g/9-oz pouch cooked jasmine rice
- 50 g/1¾ oz shelled edamame, thawed if frozen
- 1 small avocado, sliced
- 1 small cucumber, sliced
- 1 spring onion/scallion, thinly sliced
- ½ tbsp chopped fresh coriander
- 1 sheet nori, torn
- olive oil, for cooking

For the sticky tempeh

- ½ tbsp sriracha
- 2 tbsp dark soy sauce (GF: tamari)
- 1½ tbsp maple syrup
- 1 tsp sesame oil
- juice of ½ lime
- 200 g/7 oz tempeh

For the sriracha dressing

- 1 tsp sriracha
- 1 tbsp thick 0–5% fat yogurt (DF/VE: soy yogurt)
- 1 tsp maple syrup

1. Start with the sticky tempeh. In a small bowl or jar, whisk together the sriracha, soy sauce, maple syrup, sesame oil and lime juice until smooth.
2. Heat a glug of olive oil in a frying pan/skillet over medium heat. Crumble the tempeh into the pan with your hands and cook for 4–5 minutes, stirring occasionally, until golden. Pour in the glaze and cook for another 1–2 minutes, letting it completely coat the tempeh. Remove from the heat.
3. Meanwhile, microwave the rice according to the packet instructions.
4. To make the dressing, whisk together the sriracha, yogurt and maple syrup in a small bowl, then add a splash of water until smooth and pourable.
5. Assemble the bowls with the rice, edamame, cucumber, avocado, sticky tempeh and spring onions. Drizzle with the sriracha dressing, scatter over coriander, tuck in the torn nori, and serve immediately.

29g PROTEIN

8g FIBRE

Future you:

- Cool and place in an airtight container, storing in the fridge for up to 3 days.
- Cool and freeze the tempeh alone for up to 2 months.
- Thaw in the fridge overnight.
- Serve cold or reheat the tempeh and rice in a pan or microwave until piping hot. Assemble the rest fresh.

Serves 4 | Prep 10 minutes | Cook 30 minutes

Stuffed Cheesy Sweet Potatoes

V
VE/O
DF/O
GF

I'd normally always choose a regular baked potato over a sweet one, but there are a few exceptions to that rule and this is one of them. The smoky bean and corn filling with tangy melty cheese is just such a match made in heaven with the sweeter flesh, especially once finished with a big dollop of protein-boosting avocado crema on top.

- 4 sweet potatoes
- 1 × 400-g/14-oz can black beans, drained and rinsed
- 1 x 200-g/7-oz can sweetcorn, drained
- 1 red (bell) pepper, finely diced
- 1–2 jalapeños, finely diced
- juice of ½ lime
- 50 g/1¾ oz/generous ½ cup coarsely grated light cheddar (DF/VE: dairy-free cheese or omit)
- salt and pepper
- olive oil, for cooking

For the avocado crema

- 1 avocado
- 50 g/1¾ oz/scant ½ cup cottage cheese (DF/VE: soy yogurt)
- a small handful of fresh coriander/cilantro
- juice of ½ lime

1 Preheat the oven to 200°C fan/220°C/425°F/gas mark 7.

2 Pierce the sweet potatoes a few times with a fork, wrap them in damp kitchen paper/paper towel and microwave on high for 8–10 minutes until just tender. Once cool enough to handle, unwrap, drizzle with olive oil and season with salt and pepper. Pop them directly on the oven rack and bake for 20 minutes until the skins are crisp.

3 Meanwhile, in a large bowl, combine the black beans, sweetcorn, red pepper, jalapeños, lime juice, half the cheese and a good pinch of salt and pepper. Set aside.

4 To make the avocado crema, blend the avocado, cottage cheese, coriander, lime juice and a pinch of salt and pepper until smooth and creamy. Set aside.

5 Once the potatoes are ready, carefully slice each one in half lengthways and scoop out the flesh into the bowl with the bean mixture, leaving a thin layer inside the skins to help them hold their shape. Switch the oven to the grill/broiler setting.

6 Mash the sweet potato flesh lightly into the bean mixture and stir to combine. Spoon the filling back into the skins, top with the remaining cheese and place under the grill for 5 minutes, or until the cheese is melted and bubbling.

7 Serve the stuffed potatoes whilst hot with generous spoonfuls of avocado crema.

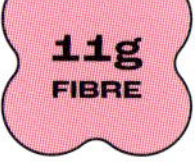

Future you:

- Cool and place in an airtight container, storing in the fridge for up to 3 days.
- Cool and freeze the stuffed potatoes (without avocado crema) for up to 2 months.
- Thaw in the fridge overnight.
- Reheat in the oven or microwave until piping hot, then top with fresh crema.

Serves 3 | Prep 13 minutes | Cook 12 minutes

Halloumi + Charred Corn Tacos

V
VE/O
DF/O
GF/O

If you've never put halloumi in a taco before, you are in for a treat. It stars one of my kitchen regulars, my charred corn salsa, which I throw into bowls or wraps and onto loaded potatoes. Paired here with creamy avocado and salty halloumi, it's a total win. Fresh, simple and on the table in under 30 minutes.

- 225 g/8 oz light halloumi, sliced into thick strips (DF/VE: extra-firm smoked tofu)
- ½ tsp smoked paprika
- ¼ tsp ground cumin
- ¼ tsp cayenne pepper
- ¼ tsp garlic granules
- ¼ tsp onion granules
- juice of ½ lime
- ¼ small white cabbage
- 6 mini tortillas (GF: corn tortillas)
- salt and pepper
- olive oil, for cooking
- 3 tbsp thick 0–5% fat yogurt (DF/VE: soy yogurt), to serve (optional)

For the salsa

- 1 x 200-g/7-oz can sweetcorn, drained
- 2 spring onions/scallions, thinly sliced
- 6 cherry tomatoes, diced
- juice of ½ lime

For the avo smash

- 1 large avocado
- juice of ½ lime
- 1 tbsp finely chopped fresh coriander/cilantro

1. Toss the halloumi with the paprika, cumin, cayenne pepper, garlic granules, onion granules, lime juice, a good pinch of salt and pepper and a teaspoon of olive oil until evenly coated.
2. Heat a drizzle of oil in a large non-stick frying pan/skillet over medium–high heat and fry the halloumi for 1–2 minutes on each side until golden and slightly crisp. Transfer to a plate and set aside.
3. Without cleaning the pan, drizzle in a little extra oil and add the corn and spring onions for the salsa. Let them sizzle for about 5 minutes, tossing occasionally so they soak up the spiced oil and pick up some colour. Tip into a bowl and stir through the diced tomatoes and lime juice. Season to taste and set aside.
4. For the avo smash, mash the avocado with the lime juice, coriander and a pinch of salt until smooth but still with some texture. Set aside.
5. Finely shred the cabbage using a mandoline or potato peeler.
6. Warm the tortillas in the same pan over medium heat until lightly blistered.
7. To assemble, spread each taco with avo smash, then pile on the shredded cabbage, warm corn salsa and halloumi. Finish with a dollop of yogurt to serve, if you like.

5g
FIBRE

Future you:

Cool and place in an airtight container, storing in the fridge for up to 2 days.
Reheat the halloumi gently in the microwave or a dry pan until warmed through. Assemble the rest fresh.

Meat + Fish

This chapter is full of some of my favourite ever recipes.

And I guarantee they will end up in your kitchen on repeat. There's everything here: comforting cheesy pasta bakes, fragrant brothy bowls and simple one-pan winners. High in protein, big on flavour and super quick to get on the table during the week.

Serves 2 | Prep 10 minutes | Cook 1 hour 15 minutes

Baked Potato With Salmon + Dill Pickle Cream

(DF/O)

You simply can't beat a loaded jacket potato – and this one is pure comfort with a little posh upgrade. It went viral on my social media for good reason: the creamy dill pickle sauce is sharp, herby and rich all at once, and pairs perfectly with the fluffy potatoes and tender salmon.

small baking sheet, lined

- 2 large baking potatoes (about 300 g/10½ oz each)
- 2 x 150-g/5¼-oz salmon fillets
- 2 tsp capers
- salt and pepper
- olive oil, for cooking

For the quick-pickled onion

- ½ small red onion, thinly sliced
- 2 tbsp white or apple cider vinegar

For the creamy dill pickle sauce

- 6 heaped tbsp crème fraîche (DF: soy-based alternative)
- 2 tsp Dijon mustard
- 4 tbsp pickles of choice, finely chopped
- 1 spring onion/scallion, finely chopped (green part only)
- 1 tbsp finely chopped fresh dill
- 1 tbsp finely chopped fresh parsley
- juice of 1 lemon

1. Preheat the oven to 210°C fan/230°C/450°F/gas mark 8.
2. Rub the potatoes all over with olive oil, salt and pepper. Prick each one a few times with a knife or fork, then wrap tightly in foil. Bake directly on the oven rack for 1 hour 15 minutes, removing the foil for the final 15 minutes so the skins can crisp up.
3. While the potatoes bake, make the quick-pickled onion. Place the sliced onion in a small bowl or jar with the vinegar and a pinch of salt. Scrunch it together with your fingers to help it soften, then set aside to pickle.
4. When the potatoes have around 10 minutes left, season the salmon with salt and pepper and place on the lined baking sheet. Bake for 8–10 minutes, or until just cooked through and flaky.
5. Meanwhile, mix the crème fraîche, mustard, chopped pickles, spring onion, dill, parsley and lemon juice in a small bowl. Season to taste.
6. To serve, cut open each potato into quarters and gently squeeze the corners to open up the flesh. Top with a generous spoonful of the pickle cream, the salmon (flaked or whole), pickled onion and capers.

Future you:

Cool and place in an airtight container, storing in the fridge for up to 3 days.
Reheat the potato and salmon in the microwave or oven until piping hot. Serve with fresh sauce and garnishes, if you can.

Serves 2 | Prep 10 minutes | Cook 20 minutes

Prawn + Anchovy Bucatini With Lemon Pangrattato

DF/O
GF/O
NF/O

This is fast, punchy pasta at its best – garlic, chilli and anchovies melted into oil, tossed with prawns, peas and bucatini. The pangrattato (a fancy name for a crunchy breadcrumb topping) adds brilliant texture and is one to keep in your arsenal for everything from pasta to salads.

- 160 g/5½ oz bucatini (GF: gluten-free pasta)
- 2 shallots, thinly sliced
- 2 big or 3 small garlic cloves, finely chopped
- 1 red chilli/chile, thinly sliced
- 3 anchovy fillets
- 100 g/3½ oz cherry tomatoes, halved
- 50 g/1¾ oz/scant ½ cup frozen petit pois
- 150 g/5¼ oz raw peeled king prawns/jumbo shrimp
- juice of ½ lemon
- 1 tbsp finely chopped fresh parsley
- salt and pepper
- olive oil, for cooking

For the pangrattato

- 20 g/¾ oz/scant ½ cup fresh or panko breadcrumbs (GF: gluten-free breadcrumbs)
- 20 g/¾ oz/2¼ tbsp walnut halves (NF: pumpkin seeds)
- 10 g/⅓ oz/2 tbsp grated Parmesan (DF: nutritional yeast)
- grated zest of ½ lemon
- 1 tbsp finely chopped parsley

1. Start by making the pangrattato. Heat 2 teaspoons of olive oil in a frying pan/skillet over medium heat. Add the breadcrumbs and toast for 3–4 minutes, stirring regularly, until golden and crisp. Season with salt and pepper.
2. Meanwhile, blitz the walnuts, Parmesan, lemon zest and parsley in a small food processor until crumbly. Tip into a bowl, stir through the toasted breadcrumbs, then set aside.
3. Bring a large pan of salted water to the boil and cook the pasta according to the packet instructions until al dente. Reserve a splash of the cooking water before draining.
4. While the pasta cooks, heat 1 tablespoon of olive oil in a large frying pan over medium heat. Add the shallots and garlic and cook for 3–4 minutes until softened. Stir in the chilli, anchovies and cherry tomatoes, and cook for another 2–3 minutes, breaking up the anchovies so they melt into the oil.
5. Add the prawns and petit pois to the pan. Cook for 2–3 minutes, or until the prawns are just pink and cooked through.
6. Add the drained pasta directly to the pan along with a splash of the reserved pasta water and the chopped parsley. Toss everything together until well coated and glossy.
7. Serve in bowls with a generous handful of the pangrattato scattered over the top and squeeze the lemon juice over.

Future you:

Cool and place in an airtight container, storing in the fridge for up to 2 days.
Reheat in a pan or microwave with a splash of water to loosen.

Serves 4 | Prep 10 minutes | Cook 20 minutes

Sun-Dried Tomato Orzo + Turkey Meatballs

I first made this for a 25-person dinner party I catered one New Year's, and it went down an absolute storm. Several of those guests asked for the recipe (sorry for the delay guys, publishing a book takes a minute!) – but here it is at last, ready for the rest of you to enjoy too. Impress with it, or eat it on the sofa on a Tuesday. It's easy enough to do both.

baking sheet, lined

- 1 onion, finely diced
- 2 garlic cloves, minced
- 150 g/5¼ oz cherry tomatoes, halved
- 80 g/2¾ oz sun-dried tomatoes, finely chopped
- 1 heaped tbsp harissa paste
- 250 g/9 oz orzo
- 600 ml/1 pint/2½ cups vegetable stock
- 1 tbsp balsamic vinegar
- 1½ tbsp light crème fraîche (DF: soy cream)
- a handful of baby spinach
- salt and pepper
- olive oil, for cooking

For the meatballs

- 500 g/1 lb 2 oz turkey thigh mince/ground turkey thigh
- 1 shallot or ¼ onion, finely diced
- 1 garlic clove, minced
- 1 egg
- 1 tsp dried oregano
- 1 tsp dried rosemary
- 20 g/¾ oz/scant ½ cup breadcrumbs
- 20 g/¾ oz/¼ cup grated Parmesan (DF: nutritional yeast), plus extra to serve

1 Preheat the oven or air fryer to 200°C fan/220°C/425°F/gas mark 7.

2 In a large bowl, combine the meatball ingredients and a generous pinch of salt and pepper. Mix well, then divide into 16 equal portions and roll into balls. Arrange on the lined baking sheet, drizzle lightly with oil, and bake or air-fry for 20 minutes, flipping halfway, until golden and cooked through.

3 Meanwhile, make the orzo. Heat a glug of olive oil in a pan over medium heat. Add the onion and garlic and cook for 2–3 minutes until softened. Stir in the cherry and sun-dried tomatoes and cook for another 3 minutes, gently squashing the tomatoes with the back of a spoon to release their juices.

4 Add the harissa paste and orzo, stir to coat, then pour in the stock. Bring to the boil, reduce the heat and simmer, covered, for about 10 minutes, stirring occasionally, until the orzo is al dente and most of the liquid has been absorbed.

5 Remove from the heat and stir through the balsamic vinegar, crème fraîche and spinach until the greens have wilted and the sauce is glossy.

6 Serve the orzo in bowls with four meatballs each, and finish with an extra grating of Parmesan and a crack of black pepper, if you like.

Future you:

- Cool and place in an airtight container, storing in the fridge for up to 3 days.
- ❄ Cool and freeze the meatballs and orzo separately for up to 2 months.
- Thaw in the fridge overnight.
- Reheat in the microwave until piping hot, adding a splash of water to loosen the orzo if needed.

Serves 3 | Prep 15 minutes | Cook 10 minutes

Prawn Katsu Burger

Prawn burgers aren't enough of a thing, and I think they should be. This one is crunchy on the outside, soft and fragrant on the inside, and dripping with tangy sriracha sauce for the perfect mouthful. Next time you fancy a burger, switch it up and make this, then thank me later.

- 3 spring onions/scallions, roughly chopped
- 1 garlic clove, roughly chopped
- 10 g/⅓ oz fresh parsley, roughly chopped
- 1 red chilli/chile
- 200 g/7 oz raw king prawns/jumbo shrimp, peeled and deveined
- 2.5-cm/1-in piece fresh ginger, peeled and grated
- 1 egg white
- 3 tbsp cornflour/cornstarch
- 50 g/1¾ oz/generous 1 cup panko breadcrumbs
- ¼ white cabbage
- 3 burger buns
- 1 avocado, sliced
- salt and pepper
- neutral oil, for cooking

For the sriracha sauce

- 3 tbsp thick 0–5% fat yogurt (DF: soy yogurt)
- 1 tbsp sriracha
- 1 tsp honey
- juice of 1 small lime

1 Add the spring onions, garlic, parsley and chilli to a food processor along with the prawns, ginger, egg white, cornflour and a good pinch of salt and pepper. Pulse until everything's finely chopped and starting to come together – you want texture, not a smooth paste.

2 Shape into three thick, chunky patties, then pour the panko breadcrumbs onto a plate and press in each patty, to coat evenly on both sides.

3 Heat 2 tablespoons of oil in a large frying pan/skillet over medium heat. Fry the burgers for 3–4 minutes per side until golden and cooked through. Transfer briefly to kitchen paper/paper towel to soak up any excess oil.

4 Meanwhile, whisk together the yogurt, sriracha, honey and lime juice to make the sauce. Depending on the thickness of your yogurt, add a splash of water to loosen to a ketchup-like consistency.

5 Finely shred the cabbage using a mandoline or peeler, then toss with half the sriracha sauce.

6 Lightly toast the burger buns, then layer up with a spoonful of sauce, avocado slices, the prawn patty and the crunchy dressed cabbage.

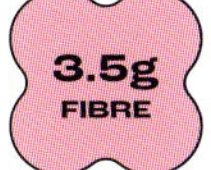

Future you:

- Cool and place in an airtight container, storing in the fridge for up to 2 days.
- Freeze the uncooked patties for up to 1 month.
- Thaw in the fridge overnight.
- Pan-fry, air-fry or re-crisp the patties in the oven until piping hot. Assemble fresh.

Serves 4 | Prep 15 minutes | Cook 25 minutes

Honey Harissa Salmon + Fennel Rice

This one was born from a fridge forage and turned into one of my favourite salmon recipes ever. It's got that perfect mix of sweet, spicy and herby flavours, with the dill, feta and lemon cutting through the richness. Everything cooks in the oven at once, which also makes it the dream midweek dinner when effort levels are low.

Baking sheet, lined

- 1 fennel bulb, cut into wedges
- 1 white onion, thinly sliced
- 2 garlic cloves, thinly sliced
- 1 tsp ground cumin
- 2 tsp za'atar
- 300 g/10½ oz/1½ cups easy-cook long-grain rice
- 450 ml/16 fl oz/scant 2 cups vegetable stock
- 1½ tbsp rose harissa
- 1 tbsp honey
- 4 salmon fillets
- juice of ½ lemon, plus ½ lemon, sliced
- 1 x 400-g/14-oz can chickpeas/garbanzo beans, drained and rinsed
- 60 g/2¼ oz feta, crumbled (DF: dairy-free feta or omit)
- 1 small bunch fresh dill, chopped
- salt and pepper
- olive oil, for cooking
- salad leaves, to serve

1 Preheat the oven to 200°c fan/220°C/425°f/gas mark 7.

2 Heat a glug of olive oil in a frying pan/skillet over medium heat. Add the fennel and onion and cook for 5–6 minutes until lightly golden. Stir in the garlic, cumin and za'atar, season generously with salt and pepper, and cook for another minute.

3 Add the rice and toast for 1 minute, stirring to coat, then transfer everything to a large ovenproof dish, pour in the stock, and cover tightly with foil. Bake on the bottom shelf of the oven for 15–20 minutes until the rice is tender and the liquid has been absorbed.

4 Meanwhile, mix the rose harissa and honey in a small bowl. Place the salmon fillets on the baking sheet, brush generously with the honey and harissa glaze, and top each fillet with a lemon slice. Bake on the top shelf of the oven for 10 minutes, or until the salmon is just cooked.

5 Once the rice is done, fluff with a fork and stir through the chickpeas, feta, dill and lemon juice. Season with salt and pepper to taste.

6 Serve the salmon fillets alongside the fennel rice, with a handful of green leaves on the side.

Future you:

Cool and place in an airtight container, storing in the fridge for up to 3 days. The salmon will be best fresh, but can be reheated gently in the microwave with the rice until both are piping hot.

Serves 2 | Prep 15 minutes | Cook 15 minutes

Cheesy Orzo With Sea Bass + Sauce Viergee

This one's a little French-Italian fusion that feels restaurant-level but takes barely half an hour to make. The sauce vierge, basically France's answer to bruschetta topping, brings so much brightness and the orzo underneath catches every last drop of the lemony, herby goodness. So good.

- 140 g/5 oz orzo (GF: gluten-free orzo)
- 20 g/¾ oz/¼ cup grated Parmesan (DF: nutritional yeast)
- 2 skin-on sea bass fillets
- salt and pepper
- olive oil, for cooking
- dressed salad leaves, to serve

For the sauce vierge

- 3 ripe tomatoes, deseeded and finely diced
- 1 shallot, finely diced or sliced
- 40 g/1½ oz/generous ⅓ cup black olives, roughly chopped
- 1 small garlic clove, finely minced
- 3 tbsp extra virgin olive oil
- grated zest and juice of ½ lemon
- 2 tbsp chopped fresh basil
- 1 tbsp chopped fresh parsley
- 1 tbsp chopped fresh chives (optional)

1. Start by making the sauce vierge. In a small bowl, combine the diced tomatoes, shallot, olives, garlic, olive oil, lemon zest and juice, basil, parsley, chives and a good pinch of salt and pepper. Stir well and set aside to let the flavours meld.

2. Bring a pan of salted water to the boil and cook the orzo according to the packet instructions until al dente. Drain, then stir through the Parmesan and plenty of black pepper.

3. Meanwhile, pat the sea bass fillets dry with kitchen paper/paper towel and season the skin-side with salt. Heat a glug of olive oil in a large non-stick frying pan/skillet over medium–high heat. Add the fish skin-side down and cook for 3–4 minutes, pressing gently with a spatula to keep the skin flat and crisp. Flip and cook for another 1–2 minutes until just cooked through.

4. To serve, spoon the orzo onto plates, top with the sea bass and finish with generous spoonfuls of the sauce vierge. A handful of dressed salad leaves on the side works beautifully too.

Future you:

Cool and place in an airtight container, storing in the fridge for up to 2 days.
Reheat the orzo gently in a pan or microwave with a splash of water, then top with fresh fish and sauce.

Serves 2 | Prep 10 minutes | Cook 20 minutes

Brothy Thai Chicken + Rice

This is what I make when I want comfort food that still feels bright and fresh. The broth is gingery and fragrant, and the rice soaks up every bit of that flavour. A simple, 30-minute high-protein meal that never fails to hit the spot.

- 2 boneless, skinless chicken thighs
- 1 tbsp Thai red curry paste
- 1 garlic clove, minced
- 2.5-cm/1-in piece fresh ginger, peeled and grated
- 300 ml/10 fl oz/1¼ cups chicken stock
- 100 ml/3½ fl oz/6½ tbsp oat or soy milk
- 1 tsp soy sauce (GF: tamari) or ½ tsp fish sauce
- 1 x 250-g/9-oz pouch cooked jasmine rice
- ¼ red onion, thinly sliced
- 1 red chilli/chile, thinly sliced
- a handful of fresh coriander/cilantro
- 1 tbsp cashews, chopped
- salt and pepper
- olive oil, for cooking
- lime wedges, to serve

1. Pat the chicken thighs dry with kitchen paper/paper towel, then season with salt and pepper.
2. Heat a drizzle of oil in a deep frying pan/skillet or shallow casserole dish over medium–high heat. Add the chicken and cook for 4–5 minutes on each side until golden and cooked through. Remove from the pan and set aside.
3. Reduce the heat to medium and add a touch more oil if needed, then stir in the curry paste, garlic and ginger. Cook for 1 minute until fragrant, then pour in the stock, oat milk and soy or fish sauce. Stir to combine and let it simmer gently for 5 minutes.
4. Meanwhile, microwave the rice according to the packet instructions. Slice the chicken into strips.
5. Spoon the rice into bowls, top with the sliced chicken and ladle the fragrant broth over the top. Finish with the red onion, chilli, coriander and cashews, and serve with lime wedges for squeezing over.

Future you:

Cool and place in an airtight container, storing in the fridge for up to 3 days.
Cool and freeze the broth and chicken for up to 2 months.
Thaw in the fridge overnight.
Reheat in a pan or microwave until piping hot, adding a splash of water if needed.

Serves 4 | Prep 10 minutes | Cook 15 minutes

Turkey Mince 'Yaki Udon'

V/O

VE/O

DF

GF/O

This is what I call a low-effort, high-reward dinner. Turkey thigh mince gives you all the protein and leanness of breast but with a little extra flavour and juiciness, which makes all the difference. Quick to throw together, full of flavour and really satisfying.

- 4 tbsp dark soy sauce (GF: tamari)
- 2 tsp rice vinegar
- 1 tbsp sesame oil
- a splash of fish sauce (V/VE: omit)
- 1 tbsp crispy chilli oil/crispy chile oil, plus extra to serve
- 150 g/5¼ oz broccoli, cut into small pieces
- 2 garlic cloves, minced
- 2.5-cm/1-in piece fresh ginger, peeled and grated
- 500 g/1 lb 2 oz turkey thigh mince/ground turkey thigh (V/VE: extra-firm tofu, crumbled)
- 4 spring onions/scallions, green only, cut into 5-cm/2-in pieces
- 2 x 200-g/7-oz packs cooked udon noodles, or 300 g/10½ oz fresh udon noodles (GF: gluten-free noodles)
- olive oil, for cooking
- sesame seeds, to serve

1. Whisk together the soy sauce, rice vinegar, sesame oil, fish sauce (if using) and crispy chilli oil in a small bowl or jug until combined. Set aside.

2. Heat a glug of olive oil in a large frying pan/skillet or wok over medium heat. Add the broccoli and let it sizzle undisturbed for 2 minutes until beginning to char in spots. Push it to one side, then add the garlic and ginger and cook for 1 minute until fragrant.

3. Crank the heat up to high and add the turkey mince. Break it up with your spoon and cook for 3–4 minutes until browned all over. Stir in the spring onions and cook for another 2–3 minutes until just softened.

4. Meanwhile, cook the noodles according to the packet instructions. Drain and set aside.

5. Going back to the wok – reduce the heat slightly, pour in the sauce and stir well. Add the noodles and toss together until everything's coated and piping hot.

6. Divide among bowls and finish with a sprinkle of sesame seeds and an extra drizzle of crispy chilli oil.

Future you:

- Cool and place in an airtight container, storing in the fridge for up to 3 days.
- Cool and freeze for up to 2 months (the noodles may soften slightly once thawed).
- Thaw in the fridge overnight.
- Reheat in a pan or microwave until piping hot, with a splash of water to loosen.

Serves 3 | Prep 15 minutes | Cook 20 minutes

Chicken Skewers with Feta + Lentil Salad

V/O

VE/O

For nights when you want something fresh but still filling, this one delivers – and happens to be a bit of a protein and fibre powerhouse too. The chicken skewers are deliciously juicy, the lentil salad brings tangy balance, and together they make a dinner that's both light and hearty.

baking sheet, lined (if using the oven)
wooden skewers, soaked for 15 minutes

- 1 tbsp olive oil
- 1 tsp dried oregano
- 1 tsp dried thyme
- ½ tsp garlic granules
- ½ tsp onion granules
- 600 g/1 lb 7 oz boneless, skinless chicken thighs, cut into bite-sized pieces (V/VE: extra-firm tofu)
- salt and pepper

For the salad

- 1 small cucumber
- 1 x 250-g/9-oz pouch cooked beluga lentils
- 1 x 400-g/14-oz can chickpeas/garbanzo beans, drained and rinsed
- 50 g/1¾ oz dill pickles, finely chopped
- ¼ red onion, finely diced
- 40 g/1½ oz feta, crumbled (DF/VE: dairy-free feta or omit)
- 2 tbsp finely chopped fresh parsley
- 1½ tbsp olive oil, plus extra to serve
- 2 tsp wholegrain mustard
- juice of ½ lemon, plus extra to serve

1. Preheat an air fryer to 200°C/400°F or oven to 200°C fan/220°C/425°F/gas mark 7 on the grill/broiler setting – positioning a rack in the upper third.
2. In a large bowl, mix the olive oil, oregano, thyme, garlic granules, onion granules, salt and pepper. Add the chicken and toss to coat evenly. Leave to marinate while you prepare the salad.
3. Slice the cucumber in half lengthways and lay each half flat on a chopping board. Smash lightly with the side of your knife or a rolling pin, just enough to crack it open. Slice into chunky pieces and add to a large bowl with the lentils, chickpeas, pickles, red onion, feta and parsley.
4. In a small jar, whisk together the olive oil, mustard and lemon juice with a pinch of salt and pepper. Pour over the salad and toss to combine.
5. Thread the chicken onto the soaked skewers. To grill/broil in the oven, place a wire rack on the prepared baking sheet, arrange the skewers on top and grill for 10–12 minutes, turning halfway, until lightly charred and cooked through. To air-fry, place in the basket and air-fry at 200°C/400°F for 12–15 minutes, shaking or turning halfway, until golden and cooked through.
6. Serve the skewers with the lentil salad, a squeeze of lemon and a drizzle of olive oil to finish.

46g PROTEIN

11g FIBRE

Future you:

- Cool and place in an airtight container, storing in the fridge for up to 3 days.
- Cool and freeze the cooked chicken for up to 2 months; the salad is best fresh.
- Thaw in the fridge overnight.
- Reheat the chicken in the air fryer or microwave until piping hot. Enjoy the salad cold or at room temperature.

Serves 2 | Prep 10 minutes | Cook 10 minutes

Prawn Fried Rice

If you ever need proof that dinner doesn't have to be complicated to be delicious, this is it. Juicy prawns, golden rice and a glossy soy-sesame sauce that coats everything perfectly. On the table in under 20 minutes and guaranteed to hit the spot.

- 150 g/5¼ oz raw king prawns/jumbo shrimp
- 2 spring onions/scallions, thinly sliced, whites and greens separated
- 1 garlic clove, minced
- 1-cm/½-in piece fresh ginger, peeled and grated
- ½ red chilli/chile, finely chopped, plus extra for serving (optional)
- 100 g/3½ oz sugar snap peas, sliced on the diagonal
- 100 g/3½ oz baby corn, sliced into thin rounds
- 3 large/US extra-large eggs, beaten
- 1 x 250 g/9-oz pouch cooked jasmine rice
- 1 tbsp chopped fresh coriander/cilantro
- a few torn fresh Thai basil leaves (optional)
- olive oil, for cooking
- lime wedges, to serve

For the sauce

- 2 tbsp soy sauce (GF: tamari)
- ½ tbsp rice vinegar
- ½ tsp fish sauce
- 1 tsp sesame oil
- ¼ tsp white pepper

1. Stir the sauce ingredients together in a small bowl and set aside.
2. Heat a glug of oil in a large wok or frying pan/skillet over high heat. Season the prawns lightly with salt and stir-fry for 1–2 minutes until just pink. Transfer to a plate and set aside.
3. Reduce the heat to medium and add another drizzle of oil, followed by the white parts of the spring onion. Cook for 2 minutes until starting to soften, then add the garlic, ginger and chilli. Stir-fry for 30 seconds until fragrant.
4. Add the sugar snap peas and baby corn and cook for 2–3 minutes until just tender but still bright. Push the vegetables to one side and pour the eggs into the empty space. Gently scramble until just set, then fold through the vegetables.
5. Turn the heat back up to high. Add the rice, breaking up any clumps, and stir-fry for 2 minutes until hot and just starting to catch. Pour in the sauce and toss until everything's coated and glossy.
6. Return the prawns to the pan and fold through. Off the heat, stir in the coriander and Thai basil, if using. Scatter over the spring onion greens and serve with lime wedges for squeezing, plus some extra red chilli if you like an extra-spicy kick.

Future you:

Cool and place in an airtight container, storing in the fridge for up to 2 days.
Reheat in a pan or microwave until piping hot.

Serves 5–6 | Prep 15 minutes | Cook 30 minutes

Squash Mac 'n' Cheese

Don't tell anyone, but this mac 'n' cheese is mostly hidden vegetables. You'd never know it though. It's still perfectly creamy, cheesy and dangerously delicious. Exactly the kind of recipe that proves *Healthy-ish High Protein* can mean both wholesome and wildly comforting.

- 1 large butternut squash, peeled and diced
- 1 onion, quartered
- a few sprigs of fresh thyme, leaves picked
- 1 whole garlic bulb, halved horizontally
- 650 g/1 lb 7 oz chicken breasts (V: omit)
- 1 small cauliflower, cut into florets
- 250 g/9 oz macaroni (GF: gluten-free pasta)
- 70 g/2½ oz/¾ cup grated Gruyère or cheddar
- 30 g/1 oz/generous 1/3 cup grated Parmesan (V: vegetarian Parmesan)
- 100 ml/3½ fl oz/6 ½ tbsp milk of choice
- 30 g/1 oz/¾ cup panko breadcrumbs (GF: gluten-free breadcrumbs)
- salt and pepper
- olive oil, for cooking

1 Preheat the oven to 200°C fan/220°C/425°F/gas mark 7.

2 Toss the squash, onion and thyme leaves with a glug of olive oil and a good pinch of salt and pepper on a large roasting tray. Drizzle the halved garlic bulb with a little oil, wrap in foil and add to the tray. Roast for 25–30 minutes until the squash is soft and lightly caramelized.

3 On a second tray, drizzle the chicken breasts and cauliflower florets with olive oil, and season with salt and pepper. Roast for 15 minutes, or until the chicken is cooked through and the cauliflower is tender. Chop both into bite-sized pieces once cool enough to handle.

4 Meanwhile, cook the pasta according to packet instructions in salted boiling water until al dente, reserving at least 200 ml/7 fl oz/scant 1 cup of the cooking water before draining.

5 For the sauce, squeeze the roasted garlic cloves from their skins into a blender with the roasted squash, onion and half the cauliflower. Add most of the Gruyère and Parmesan (reserving a handful for topping), the milk and a good pinch of salt and pepper. Blend until smooth, then loosen with about 200 ml/7 fl oz/scant 1 cup of the reserved pasta water, adding more if needed.

6 Preheat the grill/broiler to high.

7 Pour the sauce into a large ovenproof dish, then stir in the pasta, chicken and remaining cauliflower until everything is coated and glossy. Top with breadcrumbs and the remaining cheese, then place under the hot grill for 5–7 minutes until golden and bubbling.

41g PROTEIN | **6.5g FIBRE**

Future you:

- Cool and place in an airtight container, storing in the fridge for up to 3 days.
- Cool and freeze for up to 2 months.
- Thaw in the fridge overnight.
- Reheat in the microwave or oven with a splash of water to loosen, if needed.

Serves 2 | Prep 10 minutes | Cook 20 minutes

Creamy Lemon Linguine + Flaked Salmon

Anything that comes together in one dish is a win in my books, and this gorgeous pasta is no exception. Creamy, herby and full of lemony brightness, it somehow manages to feel both comforting and light.

20 x 30-cm/8 x 12-in baking dish

- 1 onion, thinly sliced
- 100 g/3½ oz asparagus, trimmed and cut into 2.5-cm/1-in pieces
- 2 garlic cloves, halved
- 2 salmon fillets
- 1 lemon, cut into slices
- 160 g/5½ oz linguine (GF: gluten-free pasta)
- 125 g/4½ oz/generous ½ cup light crème fraîche (DF: soy cream)
- 1 tbsp finely chopped fresh dill
- 1 tbsp finely chopped fresh parsley
- ½ tsp chilli flakes/chile flakes
- salt and pepper
- olive oil, for cooking
- dressed salad leaves, to serve (optional)

1. Preheat the oven to 200°C fan/220°C/425°F/gas mark 7.
2. Add the sliced onion, asparagus and garlic cloves to the baking dish. Drizzle with a little olive oil, season with salt and pepper, and toss to coat. Spread everything into an even layer.
3. Nestle the salmon fillets into the veg and drizzle with a touch more oil. Season generously with salt and pepper, then tuck the lemon slices around the dish, reserving two to sit on top of each fillet. Bake for 15 minutes, or until the salmon is just cooked through and flakes easily.
4. Meanwhile, cook the pasta according to the packet instructions in a large pot of salted boiling water until al dente. Reserve 100 ml/3½ fl oz/6½ tbsp of the pasta water before draining.
5. Once the salmon is out of the oven, use a fork to flake it gently into chunks right in the baking dish, discarding the skin if present. Squash the garlic cloves with the back of your fork, and use tongs to squeeze some juice from the roasted lemon slices. Discard the rinds, or save a few for a garnish.
6. Add the drained pasta, crème fraîche, reserved pasta water, chopped herbs and chilli flakes straight into the dish. Toss gently until everything is coated in the creamy sauce and the veg is evenly distributed. Serve straight away with an extra crack of black pepper and a side salad, if you fancy.

Future you:

- Cool and place in an airtight container, storing in the fridge for up to 2 days.
- Cool and freeze for up to 2 months.
- Thaw in the fridge overnight.
- Reheat in the microwave with a splash of water, stirring halfway, until hot.

Serves 4 | Prep 10 minutes | Cook 25 minutes

Chicken with Tomato Rice

V/O
VE/O
DF/O
GF

This is chicken and rice on another level. The rich, tomato rice cooks all in one pan, soaking up every bit of flavour, and the creamy, tangy cucumber salad on the side cuts through everything perfectly. It's simple food done really, really well – one of my personal favourites in this book.

- 650 g/1 lb 7 oz skinless, boneless chicken thighs (V/VE: extra-firm tofu, diced)
- 1 tsp dried oregano
- salt and pepper
- olive oil, for cooking

For the tomato rice

- ½ large onion, finely diced
- 1 red (bell) pepper, finely diced
- 1 green (bell) pepper, finely diced
- 75 g/2¾ oz sun-dried tomatoes, finely chopped
- 2 garlic cloves, minced
- ½ tsp ground cumin
- 1 tsp smoked paprika
- ½ tsp chilli flakes/chile flakes
- 300 g/10½ oz/1½ cups easy-cook rice
- 500 g/1 lb 2 oz passata/strained tomatoes
- 350 ml/12 fl oz/1½ cups chicken stock (V/VE: vegetable stock)

For the salad

- 50 g/1¾ oz/scant ¼ cup thick 0–5% fat yogurt (DF/VE: soy yogurt)
- ½ tsp dijon mustard
- juice of ½ lemon
- ½ tsp honey (VE: maple syrup)
- 1 tbsp chopped fresh parsley
- 1 small cucumber, thinly sliced

1. Season the chicken thighs with oregano, salt and pepper. Heat a glug of olive oil in a large frying pan/skillet over medium–high heat and fry the chicken for 4–5 minutes per side until golden and cooked through. Remove and set aside.
2. Meanwhile, heat another glug of olive oil in a large saucepan over medium heat. Add the onion and cook for 2 minutes, then stir in the peppers, sun-dried tomatoes, garlic and spices. Cook for another 2–3 minutes until fragrant.
3. Stir in the rice and cook for 1 minute to coat. Pour in the passata and chicken stock, season, then cover and simmer for 15 minutes, stirring occasionally, until the rice is tender and the liquid has been mostly absorbed.
4. While the rice cooks, make the cucumber salad. Mix the yogurt, mustard, lemon juice, honey, parsley and a pinch of salt and pepper in a small bowl, then stir through the sliced cucumber.
5. Fluff the tomato rice with a fork and serve up with the chicken and cucumber salad.

Future you:

- Cool and place in an airtight container, storing in the fridge for up to 3 days.
- Cool and freeze the chicken and rice separately for up to 2 months.
- Thaw in the fridge overnight.
- Reheat in the microwave or a pan with a splash of water until piping hot.

Serves 4 | Prep 10 minutes | Cook 20 minutes

Smashed Caesar Tacos

This is what happens when two great things collide: Caesar salad (arguably the best salad ever) and smashed tacos. Juicy golden mince, sharp Parmesan dressing and crunchy lettuce, all wrapped up in a warm tortilla. Absolute heaven.

- 500 g/1 lb 2 oz turkey or chicken mince/ground turkey or chicken
- juice of 1 lemon
- 2 garlic cloves, minced
- 1 tsp smoked paprika
- 1 tsp dried oregano
- 8 mini tortillas (GF: corn tortillas)
- 1 romaine lettuce
- salt and pepper
- olive oil, for cooking

For the caesar dressing

- 50 g/1¾ oz/scant ¼ cup thick 0–5% fat yogurt (DF: soy yogurt)
- 2 anchovy fillets
- 15 g/½ oz/3 tbsp grated Parmesan, plus extra to serve (DF: nutritional yeast)
- 1 tsp extra virgin olive oil
- 1 tsp Dijon mustard
- 1 tsp worcestershire sauce (optional)

1. Start by making the Caesar dressing. To a small blender, add the yogurt, anchovies, Parmesan, olive oil, mustard, worcestershire sauce (if using), 1 tablespoon of water and a pinch of salt and pepper. Blitz until smooth, then set aside.
2. In a large mixing bowl, combine the mince with the lemon juice, garlic, paprika, oregano and a generous pinch of salt and pepper. Mix well to combine.
3. Lay out the tortillas on a clean surface. Divide the mince mixture among them and use a fork or your hands to press it into a thin, even layer over each one.
4. You'll need to cook these in batches – if you've got two large frying pans/skillets, now's the time to use them! Heat a drizzle of oil in each over medium heat. Once hot, place the tacos mince-side down and cook for about 4 minutes until golden and crisp. Flip and cook for 1 minute more on the other side.
5. Meanwhile, chop the romaine into chunky ribbons and toss with the caesar dressing.
6. Pile the dressed lettuce into the centre of each taco and finish with an extra grating of Parmesan. Serve while hot and crispy.

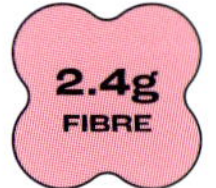

2.4g FIBRE

Future you:

- Cool tacos and place in an airtight container, storing in the fridge for up to 3 days. Keep the lettuce and dressing separate to prevent sogginess.
- For best results, reheat in a dry frying pan or air fryer for a few minutes until hot and crispy. Add the salad fresh.

Serves 2 | Prep 10 minutes | Cook 20 minutes

Pan-fried Sea Bass + Garlic Rice

Every year since I was little, I've spent time on the Portuguese coast and eaten my bodyweight in the freshest seafood. This dish is my homage to those simple, perfect meals, complete with a chickpea salad I first fell in love with at our local fish restaurant out there. Proof that less really is more.

- 2 sea bass fillets, skin on
- salt and pepper
- olive oil, for cooking
- lemon wedges, to serve

For the garlic rice

- 2–3 garlic cloves, thinly sliced
- 125 g/4½ oz/⅔ cup easy-cook rice
- 250 ml/9 fl oz/1 cup chicken or vegetable stock

For the chickpea salad

- 1 x 400-g/14-oz can chickpeas/garbanzo beans, drained and rinsed
- ½ red (bell) pepper, finely diced
- 1 small shallot, finely chopped
- 1 small garlic clove, minced
- 1 tbsp chopped fresh parsley
- 1 tbsp olive oil
- 1 tsp red or white wine vinegar

1. Start by making the rice. Heat a glug of olive oil in a saucepan over medium heat, then add the sliced garlic. Let it sizzle gently for 2–3 minutes until fragrant and just turning golden (don't let it burn). Tip in the rice, stir to coat, then pour in the stock. Bring to the boil, then reduce the heat to low, cover, and simmer for 12–15 minutes, or until the rice is cooked and the liquid has been absorbed. Fluff with a fork and season lightly with salt and pepper.

2. Meanwhile, combine the chickpea salad ingredients with a good pinch of salt and pepper in a mixing bowl. Toss well and set aside to marinate while you cook the fish.

3. Pat the sea bass fillets dry with kitchen paper/paper towels and season well with salt and pepper. Heat a drizzle of olive oil in a large non-stick frying pan/skillet over medium–high heat. Place the fillets skin-side down and cook undisturbed for 3–4 minutes until the skin is crisp and golden. Flip and cook for another 1–2 minutes until just cooked through.

4. Serve the sea bass over the garlicky rice, with a generous spoonful of chickpea salad on the side. Finish with a drizzle of olive oil and serve with lemon wedges.

Future you:

Best eaten fresh, but leftovers can be cooled and placed in an airtight container, storing in the fridge for up to 2 days.

Reheat the rice gently in the microwave with a splash of water until steaming hot. Cook the fish and assemble the salad fresh.

Serves 2 | Prep 15 minutes | Cook 15 minutes

Spiced Chicken Flatbreads with Pineapple Jalapeño Salsa

DF/O

This one's basically summer on top of a flatbread. Juicy spiced chicken, a punchy pineapple-jalapeño salsa, and all those leftover pan spices soaked up by speedy homemade flatbreads. It's fresh, fast and properly tasty.

- 3 boneless, skinless chicken thighs (V/VE: extra-firm tofu, cubed)
- ½ tsp cayenne pepper
- 1 tsp smoked paprika
- ½ tsp ground cumin
- salt and pepper
- olive oil, for cooking
- lime wedges, to serve

For the salsa

- 200 g/7 oz canned pineapple chunks, finely diced
- ½ small red onion, finely diced
- 1 jalapeño, finely diced
- juice of 1 lime
- 1 tbsp chopped fresh coriander/cilantro, plus extra to serve

For the flatbreads

- 100 g/3½ oz/¾ cup self-raising/self-rising flour
- 85 g/3 oz/generous ⅓ cup thick 0–5% fat yogurt (DF/VE: soy yogurt), plus extra to serve

1 Start with the salsa. Combine the pineapple, red onion, jalapeño, lime juice, coriander and a pinch of salt in a small bowl. Mix well and set aside to let the flavours develop.

2 In another bowl, toss the chicken thighs with the cayenne, smoked paprika, cumin, a pinch of salt and pepper and a drizzle of olive oil until evenly coated. Set aside while you make the flatbreads.

3 Mix the flour, yogurt and a pinch of salt in a bowl until a dough forms. Bring it together with your hands, then knead lightly on a floured surface for 1–2 minutes until smooth. Divide into 2 balls and roll each into a thin oval.

4 Heat a drizzle of oil in a large frying pan/skillet over medium–high heat. Once hot, add the chicken and cook for 4–5 minutes per side until golden and cooked through. Transfer to a board to rest.

5 Keep the pan over the heat and add the flatbread dough straight in – they'll soak up all those leftover chicken spices. Cook for 1–2 minutes per side until puffed and golden.

6 To serve, spread a dollop of yogurt over each flatbread, then slice the chicken and layer it on top. Spoon over the salsa, finish with extra coriander and serve with lime wedges for squeezing.

Future you:

- Cool and place in an airtight container, storing in the fridge for up to 3 days.
- Cool and freeze cooked flatbreads for up to 2 months.
- Thaw at room temperature for 30 minutes, or in the fridge overnight.
- Reheat flatbreads in a dry pan; microwave the chicken until hot. Assemble the rest fresh.

Serves 4 | Prep 10 minutes | Cook 10 minutes

Fragrant Fishcakes + Mango Salad

If you're not already cooking with canned fish, this might just convert you. Quick, protein-packed and full of flavour, these spicy, herby salmon cakes are the easiest way to make a healthy-ish dinner that still feels fresh and exciting.

- 2 x 160-g/5½-oz cans boneless, skinless salmon (or your favourite canned fish)
- 1 tbsp Thai red curry paste
- 2 spring onions/scallions, thinly sliced
- 1 garlic clove, minced
- 2.5-cm/1-in piece fresh ginger, peeled and grated
- 1 egg
- 1 x 250-g/9-oz pouch cooked quinoa
- salt and pepper
- neutral oil, for cooking

For the mango salad

- 1 ripe mango, julienned
- ½ small red onion, thinly sliced
- 1 red chilli/chile, thinly sliced
- 1 tbsp fresh mint, roughly chopped
- 1 tbsp fresh coriander/cilantro, roughly chopped
- juice of 1 lime
- 1 tsp sesame seeds

1 Add the canned salmon, curry paste, spring onions, garlic, ginger, egg, quinoa and a pinch of salt and pepper to a large bowl. Mix until well combined – the mixture should hold together when pressed. Divide into 8 portions and shape into patties.

2 Heat a glug of oil in a large non-stick frying pan/skillet over medium heat. Fry the fishcakes for 3 minutes on each side until golden and lightly crisp. Be careful not to overcook – they will dry out if left too long.

3 Meanwhile, toss the mango, red onion, chilli, mint leaves, coriander and lime juice together in a bowl. Sprinkle with the sesame seeds and season with a pinch of salt.

4 Serve the fishcakes warm with the salad piled on top or alongside.

Future you:

- Cool and place in an airtight container, storing in the fridge for up to 3 days.
- Cool and freeze the fishcakes for up to 2 months.
- Thaw in the fridge overnight.
- Reheat the fishcakes in a pan, oven or air fryer until hot all the way through.

34g PROTEIN

6g FIBRE

Serves 2 | Prep 10 minutes | Cook 30 minutes

Harissa Cod Traybake with Herby Yogurt

Nothing beats a one-tray dinner, especially when it tastes this good. Zero skill required and minimal washing up. A traybake is all about balance: you want something starchy, something saucy and something fresh to finish. This one's got it all – golden potatoes, juicy veg and flaky harissa cod, finished with herby yogurt for that final lift. Effortless, vibrant and full of protein.

- 400 g/14 oz baby potatoes
- 1 red (bell) pepper, cut into chunks
- 1 small red onion, cut into wedges
- ½ tsp smoked paprika
- ½ tsp garlic granules
- ½ tsp dried oregano
- 2 tbsp harissa paste
- 60 g/2¼ oz cherry tomatoes
- 30 g/1 oz feta, crumbled (DF: dairy-free feta or omit)
- a small handful Kalamata olives
- 2 cod fillets
- salt and pepper
- olive oil, for cooking
- dressed salad leaves, to serve

For the herby yogurt

- 75 g/2¾ oz/⅓ cup thick 0–5% fat yogurt (DF: soy yogurt)
- 1 tbsp finely chopped fresh dill
- 1 tbsp finely chopped fresh parsley
- juice of ½ lemon

1. Preheat the oven to 220°C fan/240°C/475°F/gas mark 9.
2. Halve any larger potatoes, then add them, with the pepper and red onion, to a large roasting tray. Sprinkle over the paprika, garlic granules, oregano, a pinch of salt and pepper and a drizzle of olive oil, and toss to coat. Roast for 15 minutes.
3. Remove from the oven, add the harissa paste and toss again to coat the veg evenly. Scatter over the cherry tomatoes, feta and olives, then return to the oven for 10 minutes.
4. Nestle the cod fillets among the vegetables, season with salt and pepper, and roast for a final 8–10 minutes until the fish is cooked and flakes easily.
5. Meanwhile, blitz the yogurt, dill, parsley, lemon juice, 2 tablespoons of water and a pinch of salt and pepper in a blender or with a stick blender until smooth and spoonable.
6. Serve the traybake with a handful of salad leaves, and drizzle generously with the herby yogurt.

Future you:

- Cool and place in an airtight container, storing in the fridge for up to 2 days.
- Cool and freeze the traybake (minus the herby yogurt) for up to 2 months.
- Thaw in the fridge overnight.
- Reheat in a hot oven or the microwave until hot throughout. Add the herby yogurt fresh.

Serves 2 | Prep 20 minutes | Cook 20 minutes

Sesame Crusted Tuna + Soba Noodles

DF

This one feels restaurant-level but comes together really fast. The trick to perfectly cooked tuna is heat, so we'll get the pan smoking hot and sear it for just 90 seconds a side for the perfect golden crust and soft, blushing middle. Paired with silky soba noodles, which are naturally high in protein and fibre, this one is ideal for a date night or just a quick weeknight dinner that feels like a treat.

- 3 tbsp soy sauce (GF: tamari)
- 2 tsp toasted sesame oil
- 2.5-cm/1-in piece fresh ginger, peeled and grated
- 1 garlic clove, crushed
- juice of 1 lime
- 2 spring onions/scallions, thinly sliced
- 2 Ahi tuna steaks
- 160 g/5½ oz soba noodles
- 1 tbsp honey
- 1 tbsp tahini
- 1 tsp rice vinegar
- 1 tbsp white sesame seeds
- 1 tbsp black sesame seeds
- ½ tsp garlic powder
- ½ tsp onion powder
- 100 g/3½ oz cooked edamame
- 1 small carrot, peeled into ribbons
- 1 tbsp coriander/cilantro leaves
- 1 red chilli/chile, thinly sliced
- salt and pepper
- neutral oil, for cooking

1 Combine the soy sauce, sesame oil, ginger, garlic, lime juice and spring onions in a shallow dish. Add the tuna steaks and leave to marinate for about 10 minutes, turning once so they're evenly coated.

2 Meanwhile, cook the soba noodles in boiling water according to the packet instructions. Drain and rinse thoroughly under cold water to remove the starch and stop them clumping together. Set aside.

3 Leaving the tuna in the dish, pour the remaining marinade into a small pan over medium heat. Stir in the honey, tahini, rice vinegar and 1–2 tablespoons of water, then simmer for 3–5 minutes until it thickens into a creamy, glossy glaze. Set aside.

4 On a plate, mix the white and black sesame seeds with the garlic powder, onion powder and a pinch of salt and pepper. Press the marinated tuna into the mixture on both sides to coat.

5 Heat a glug of neutral oil in a large non-stick frying pan/skillet over medium-high heat and sear the tuna for 1–1½ minutes on each side, or until cooked to your liking. Transfer to a board.

6 Pour the reduced glaze into the same pan off the heat, then add the noodles. Toss for a minute or two until coated and sticky, then throw in the edamame and carrot ribbons and toss to combine.

7 Serve the noodles topped with the tuna and scatter the coriander and red chilli on top.

Future you:

Store in the fridge for up to 2 days.
Enjoy cold, or gently reheat the noodles only in the microwave or a pan with a splash of water to loosen the glaze.

Serves 2 | Prep 10 minutes | Cook 25 minutes

Smoky Chipotle Lentils with Squash + Pan-Fried Salmon

V/O
VE/O

DF/O
GF/O

A hearty dinner without being heavy. The smoky lentils do all the flavour lifting, the roasted squash brings sweetness, and the sharp lime yogurt balances it all. It looks like effort, tastes like effort, but it's secretly low effort – which is always the goal.

baking sheet, lined

- 400 g/14 oz butternut squash, cubed
- ½ tsp smoked paprika
- 1 onion, finely chopped
- 2 garlic cloves, minced
- 1 tsp ground cumin
- ½ tsp smoked paprika
- 1 tbsp chipotle paste
- 1 tbsp tomato purée/paste
- 1 × 250-g/9-oz pouch cooked beluga lentils
- 200 ml/7 fl oz/scant 1 cup vegetable stock
- 1 tsp dark soy sauce (GF: tamari)
- juice of ½ lime
- 2 salmon fillets (V/VE: extra-firm tofu, cubed)
- 1 tbsp chopped fresh coriander/cilantro
- 1 tbsp pumpkin seeds
- salt and pepper
- olive oil, for cooking

For the lime yogurt

- 80 g/2¾ oz/generous ⅓ cup thick 0–5% fat yogurt (DF/VE: soy yogurt)
- grated zest and juice of ½ lime

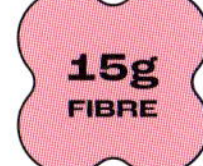

1. Preheat the oven to 200°C fan/220°C/425°F/gas mark 7.
2. Toss the squash with a glug of olive oil, the smoked paprika and a pinch of seasoning and spread evenly on the lined baking sheet. Roast for 25 minutes, turning once, until golden and tender.
3. Heat a glug of olive oil in a frying pan/skillet over medium heat. Add the onion and cook for about 5 minutes, stirring often, until softened. Stir in the garlic, cumin, smoked paprika, chipotle paste and tomato purée, and cook for 1 minute until fragrant.
4. Pour in the lentils, stock, soy sauce and lime juice. Season, then simmer gently for 5 minutes until thickened. Take off the heat.
5. Meanwhile, mix the yogurt with the lime zest and juice, plus just enough water to loosen to a drizzling consistency. Season lightly with salt and pepper and set aside.
6. In another non-stick frying pan, heat a drizzle of olive oil over medium–high heat. Pat the salmon dry and season well. Cook, undisturbed, skin-side down for 3–4 minutes until crisp, then flip and cook for 1–2 minutes until just cooked through.
7. When the squash is ready, fold it through the smoky lentils.
8. Spoon the lentils into two bowls, top with the salmon, drizzle over the lime yogurt and finish with the coriander and pumpkin seeds.

Future you:

Cool and place in an airtight container, storing in the fridge for up to 3 days.
Cool and freeze the lentils for up to 2 months. The salmon and drizzle are best fresh.
Thaw in the fridge overnight.
Reheat the lentils in a microwave or pan with a splash of water. Add the rest fresh.

Sweets

Sweet tooths, assemble!

This chapter is all about delicious sweet things that feel indulgent but still leave you feeling good. I spent a long time on these to make sure protein and fibre never came at the expense of taste. So no, these are not a million grams of protein each – and honestly, you should thank me for that. There is no need. They're simply satisfying, dangerously good and guaranteed to hit the spot.

Serves 8 | Prep 15 minutes | Cook 35 minutes, plus 2 hours chilling time

Lemon Cheesecake

I put this cheesecake in front of my harshest critics (my family) and no one guessed it was mostly cottage cheese and yogurt – my dad probably wouldn't have eaten it had he known, but the sucker was duped! It's creamy, tangy and lush, just like a 'proper' cheesecake, but with a healthy-ish twist.

20-cm/8-in springform cake tin/pan, base-lined

For the base

- 150 g/5¼ oz/1½ cups ground almonds
- 40 g/1½ oz/generous ¼ cup oat flour (GF: check label)
- a pinch of salt
- grated zest of 1 lemon
- 2½ tbsp coconut oil, melted
- 2 tbsp honey

For the filling

- 270 g/9½ oz/1¼ cups cottage cheese
- 270 g/9½ oz/1¼ cups 5% fat Greek yogurt
- 90 g/3 oz/generous ⅓ cup low-fat cream cheese
- grated zest and juice of 1 lemon
- 1 egg
- 1 tbsp cornflour/cornstarch
- 3 tbsp honey

For the blueberry compote

- 200 g/7 oz frozen blueberries
- 1½ tbsp honey

1 Preheat the oven to 170°C fan/190°C/375°F/gas mark 5.

2 In a mixing bowl, stir together the ground almonds, oat flour, salt and lemon zest. Add the melted coconut oil and honey, then mix until the texture resembles damp sand. Tip into the prepared tin and press down evenly with the back of a spoon. Bake for 12 minutes, or until lightly golden. Set aside to cool slightly.

3 Meanwhile, make the filling. Add the cottage cheese, yogurt, cream cheese, lemon zest and juice, egg, cornflour and honey to a blender. Blitz until completely smooth.

4 Pour the filling over the cooled base and tap the tin gently to level. Bake for 35–40 minutes, or until the edges are set and the centre still has a gentle wobble. Turn off the oven, open the door just a crack, and leave the cheesecake inside for 45 minutes–1 hour to cool gradually.

5 Remove from the oven and leave to cool to room temperature in the tin. Once cool, transfer to the fridge for at least 2 hours (ideally overnight) to set fully.

6 For the blueberry compote, place the blueberries and honey in a small pan over medium heat. Cook for 4–5 minutes, stirring occasionally, until the berries have softened and released their juices but still hold some shape.

7 Slice the chilled cheesecake and serve with a spoonful of the blueberry compote.

2.3g
FIBRE

Future you:

- Cool and place in an airtight container, storing in the fridge for up to 4 days.
- Cool and freeze the cheesecake (whole or in slices) for up to 1 month.
- Thaw in the fridge overnight.
- Serve the cheesecake chilled. Reheat the compote gently in a small pan or microwave.

Serves 4 | Prep 20 minutes, plus freezing | Cook 10 minutes

Raspberry Ripple Frozen Yogurt

V
VE/O
GF
DF/O
NF/O

The hardest thing about DIY frozen yogurt is getting it to be creamy rather than icy, but this ice-cube-tray method does a fantastic job. Add in a tangy raspberry ripple, toasted almonds and a molten chocolate pour, and we're firmly in proper pudding territory. The base is endlessly adaptable, so get experimenting with flavours and pair it with other puds.

- 400 g/14 oz/1¾ cups 5% fat Greek yogurt (DF/VE: soy yogurt)
- 200 ml/scant 1 cup full-fat coconut milk
- 80 g/2¾ oz/generous ¼ cup honey (VE: maple syrup)
- 1 tsp vanilla extract
- 20 g/¾ oz/¼ cup flaked/slivered almonds (NF: omit)
- 40 g/1½ oz dark/bittersweet chocolate

For the ripple

- 150 g/5¼ oz frozen raspberries
- ½ tbsp honey (VE: maple syrup)
- 1 tbsp chia seeds

1 Blend the yogurt, coconut milk, honey and vanilla extract until smooth. Pour into a silicone ice-cube tray (you may need more than one) and freeze for at least 4 hours, or until solid.

2 Once frozen, pop the cubes out into a high-speed blender and blend until smooth and creamy. Transfer to an airtight container and freeze for 1 hour.

3 Meanwhile, make the raspberry ripple. Place the raspberries, honey and chia seeds in a small pan over medium heat. Cook for 4–5 minutes, stirring often, until the berries break down and release their juices. Leave to cool completely – it will thicken up as it cools.

4 Toast the flaked almonds in a dry frying pan/skillet over medium heat for 3–4 minutes, tossing often, until golden. Leave to cool.

5 Remove the frozen yogurt from the freezer and stir to break up any ice crystals. Fold in the almonds, then dollop the cooled raspberry mixture over the top and swirl through with the handle of a spoon to create a ripple effect. Return to the freezer to set completely.

6 When serving, melt the dark chocolate in short bursts in the microwave. Let the frozen yogurt sit at room temperature for 5–10 minutes to thaw, then scoop into bowls and drizzle with the molten chocolate so it sets on contact.

Future you:

Store in an airtight container in the freezer for up to 3 weeks. After that, you may need to re-blend.
Allow to sit at room temperature for 5–10 minutes before scooping. Melt the chocolate just before serving.

Serves 4 | Prep 10 minutes | Chill 2 hours

Chocolate Orange Mousse

V
VE/O
GF
DF/O

A secret source of protein and dairy-free, thanks to the magic of silken tofu. It might sound odd if you've never tried it before, but trust me, it's a winner. The tofu is completely flavourless and transforms into a velvety, high-protein cream when blended, creating the perfect base to carry the rich choc-orange flavours.

- 1 x 300-g/10½-oz block silken tofu
- 1 tbsp maple syrup
- grated zest and juice of ½ orange, plus extra zest to serve
- 1 tbsp cacao powder
- 100 g/3½ oz dark/bittersweet chocolate, melted and cooled slightly, plus extra, grated, to serve
- thick 0–5% fat yogurt (DF/VE: soy yogurt), to serve

1. To a blender, add the tofu, maple syrup, orange zest and juice, cacao powder and melted chocolate. Blend until completely smooth and glossy.

2. Divide the mixture among cocktail glasses or small bowls, then chill for at least 2 hours until thickened and mousse-like. The longer it chills, the richer it becomes.

3. When ready to serve, top with a dollop of yogurt and a sprinkle of grated chocolate and orange zest.

3.5g
FIBRE

Future you:

Cool and place in an airtight container, storing in the fridge for up to 4 days.

Serves 9 | Prep 10 minutes | Cook 20 minutes

Chickpea Blondies

V
VE/O
GF
DF/O
NF/O

When I first started writing this book, I was determined not to put pulses or tofu in too many weird places... But once I had given these a try, I'm sorry, that promise went out the window. You're going to have to trust that they don't taste like chickpeas at all – just rich, fudgy and sweet with a sneaky hit of protein and fibre.

17-cm/7-in square tin/pan, lined (allow the paper to overhang the edges)

- 1 x 400-g/14-oz can chickpeas/garbanzo beans, drained and rinsed
- 90 g/3 oz/6½ tbsp runny peanut butter (NF: tahini)
- 3 tbsp thick 0–5% fat yogurt (DF/VE: soy yogurt)
- 25 g/1 oz/¼ cup ground almonds (NF: oat flour)
- 70 ml/2½ fl oz/5 tablespoons maple syrup
- ½ tbsp vanilla extract
- ¼ tsp baking powder
- ¼ tsp bicarbonate of soda/baking soda
- ½ tsp fine sea salt
- 45 g/1½ oz/generous ¼ cup dark/bittersweet chocolate chips, plus extra to top
- a pinch of flaky sea salt, to top (optional)

1 Preheat the oven to 180°C fan/200°C/400°F/gas mark 6.

2 Add all the ingredients except the chocolate chips to a food processor and blend until completely smooth. The mixture will be thick, but it should still be pourable.

3 Tip in the chocolate chips and pulse a few times to evenly distribute them without breaking them up.

4 Pour the batter into the prepared tin and use the back of a spoon to smooth out the top. Sprinkle over a few extra chocolate chips and press them in gently.

5 Bake on the middle shelf of the oven for 20 minutes until puffed and golden on top. A cocktail stick/toothpick inserted into the centre should come out mostly clean – a few crumbs are fine.

6 Leave the blondies to cool in the tin for 20 minutes before removing and slicing into squares. Finish with a pinch of flaky salt across the top, if you like.

Future you:

- Store in an airtight container at room temperature for up to 3 days, or in the fridge for up to 5 days.
- Cool and insert a piece of parchment paper between each blondie. Stack and freeze for up to 2 months.
- Thaw in the fridge overnight.
- Enjoy at room temperature, or warm in the microwave for a few seconds.

Serves 8 | Prep 15 minutes | Cook 50 minutes

Pear, Honey + Almond Cake

GF/O

N

Moist, nutty and gently sweet, this cake feels effortlessly special, while still being wholesome enough for any day of the week. I love it with a dollop of yogurt and extra drizzle of honey, but ice cream or a drizzle of cream would be just as dreamy – especially if you're serving it for an occasion.

23-cm/9-in springform cake tin/pan, lined

- 200 g/7 oz/2 cups ground almonds
- 100 g/3½ oz/¾ cup plain/all-purpose flour (GF: gluten-free flour)
- 1½ tsp baking powder
- ¼ tsp bicarbonate of soda/baking soda
- ½ tsp fine sea salt
- 1½ tsp ground cinnamon
- ½ tsp ground ginger
- 2 large/US extra-large eggs
- 1 pear, grated and excess water squeezed out (about 100 g/3½ oz), plus 1 pear, cored and thinly sliced
- 100 g/3½ oz/6 tbsp honey, plus extra to glaze
- 120 g/4 oz/generous ½ cup thick 0–5% fat yogurt (DF: soy yogurt)
- 60 ml/2 fl oz/¼ cup olive oil
- 1 tsp vanilla extract
- ½ tsp almond extract
- 25 g/¾ oz/¼ cup flaked/slivered almonds

1. Preheat the oven to 160°C fan/180°C/350°F/gas mark 4.
2. In a large bowl, whisk together the ground almonds, flour, baking powder, bicarbonate of soda, salt, cinnamon and ginger.
3. In a separate bowl, whisk together the eggs, grated pear, honey, yogurt, olive oil, vanilla and almond extract until smooth.
4. Add the dry ingredients to the wet and fold until just combined, being careful not to overmix. Pour the batter into the prepared tin and gently spread it to the edges. Arrange the pear slices over the top in a fan shape and scatter over the flaked almonds.
5. Slide the tin onto the middle shelf of the oven and bake for about 50 minutes, or until a knife inserted into the centre comes out mostly clean (a little moisture from the pear is fine).
6. While still warm, drizzle about a tablespoon of honey over the top to glaze, gently brushing it over the surface to cover. Allow to cool in the tin for 10 minutes, then transfer to a wire rack to cool completely.

11g PROTEIN

5g FIBRE

Future you:

- Store in an airtight container at room temperature for up to 3 days, or in the fridge for up to 5 days.
- Slice and freeze slices individually for up to 2 months.
- Thaw at room temperature, or in the fridge overnight.
- Enjoy at room temperature, or warm in the microwave for a few seconds.

Serves 4 | Prep 10 minutes | Cook 40 minutes

Pistachio Rice Pudding with Roasted Cherries

V

VE/O

GF

DF/O

NF/O

I hope you've experienced the joy of rice pudding and jam at least once in your life. This is my grown-up take with all the same cosy comfort, except with pistachios, orange and glossy roasted cherries on top. It's nostalgic, nourishing and, luckily for this book, a secret boost of protein, too.

- 150 g/5¼ oz/generous ¾ cup pudding rice
- 700 ml/1¼ pints/scant 3 cups semi-skimmed milk (DF/VE: oat or soy milk)
- 15 g/½ oz/2 tbsp raisins
- 40 ml/1½ fl oz/2½ tbsp maple syrup
- 1 tsp vanilla extract
- ½ tsp ground cinnamon
- grated zest of 1 orange
- a pinch of fine sea salt
- 40 g/1½ oz/scant ½ cup shelled pistachios (NF: omit), plus extra to serve
- 200 g/7 oz cherries, pitted
- juice of ½ orange
- 120 g/4 oz/generous ½ cup thick 0–5% fat yogurt (DF/VE: soy yogurt)

1 Preheat the oven to 180°C fan/200°C/400°F/gas mark 6.

2 Add the rice to a medium saucepan with the milk, 200 ml/7 fl oz/scant 1 cup of water, the raisins, maple syrup, vanilla, cinnamon, orange zest and salt. Bring to the boil, then lower the heat and simmer gently for about 40 minutes, stirring every now and then (especially at the beginning and end), until the rice is tender and the mixture is thick and creamy.

3 Meanwhile, blitz the pistachios in a small food processor until they resemble fine crumbs, then set aside.

4 Spread the cherries out on a baking sheet and squeeze over the orange juice. Roast for 20 minutes until soft and jammy.

5 Once the rice is done, take it off the heat and stir in the ground pistachios. Let it cool slightly, then fold through the yogurt until smooth and creamy.

6 Serve warm or chilled, topped with the roasted cherries and a few extra pistachios, if you like.

Future you:

Cool and place in an airtight container, storing in the fridge for up to 4 days.

Enjoy cold, or reheat gently on the hob or in the microwave with a splash of milk to loosen.

Serves 6-8 | Prep 10 minutes | Cook 30 minutes

Self-Saucing Chocolate Pudding

Prepare yourself for the absolute heaven that is a rich, gooey chocolate pudding that magically makes its own sauce in the oven. Think somewhere between a molten cake and a brownie, except lighter and a whole lot easier. Best eaten warm with a big scoop of my Raspberry Ripple Frozen Yogurt (see page 174).

20-cm/8-in square baking dish

- 150 g/5¼ oz/generous 1 cup plain/all-purpose flour
- 75 g/2¾ oz/scant ½ cup coconut sugar
- 2 tsp baking powder
- 25 g/1 oz/¼ cup unsweetened cocoa powder
- ¼ tsp fine sea salt
- 125 ml/4½ fl oz/½ cup milk of choice
- 60 ml/2 fl oz/¼ cup coconut oil, melted
- 40 ml/1½ fl oz/2½ tbsp maple syrup
- ½ tsp vanilla extract
- ice cream or Raspberry Ripple Frozen yogurt (see page 174), to serve

For the sauce

- 20 g/¾ oz/scant ¼ cup unsweetened cocoa powder
- 60 g/2¼ oz/generous ⅓ cup coconut sugar
- 400 ml/14 fl oz/1¾ cups boiling water

1 Preheat the oven to 170°C fan/190°C/375°F/gas mark 5.

2 In a large bowl, whisk together the flour, coconut sugar, baking powder, cocoa powder and salt.

3 In a separate bowl or jug, mix the milk, coconut oil, maple syrup and vanilla until smooth.

4 Gradually pour the wet ingredients into the dry, stirring until just combined, then pour the batter into the prepared baking dish and smooth the top with a flat rubber spatula.

5 In a small bowl, combine the cocoa powder and coconut sugar for the sauce, then sprinkle evenly over the top of the batter – don't stir it in.

6 Gently and carefully pour the boiling water over the back of a serving spoon so it settles evenly over the sugared surface without disturbing it too much. Even if it looks a mess, just trust the process!

7 Bake for 25–30 minutes, until the top is set and springy to the touch but there's a rich, gooey sauce bubbling underneath.

8 Serve straight away (the sauce thickens as it cools, so don't wait too long!) with a scoop of frozen yogurt or ice cream.

Future you:

Cool and place in an airtight container, storing in the fridge for up to 3 days.
Reheat portions in the microwave for 30 seconds until warm and saucy again.

Serves 12 | Prep 20 minutes, plus setting | Cook 15 minutes

Salted Caramel Millionaire Bars

V
VE
GF

DF
N

These are *seriously* good. Just as rich, gooey and chocolate-topped as the classic millionaire shortbread you grew up with, only made with better-for-you ingredients that still deliver all the satisfaction. The chickpea flour adds a subtle nuttiness to the base and a surprising boost of protein (also the slight yellow-ish tinge), making these bars that rare thing – indulgent yet genuinely nourishing.

900-g/2-lb loaf tin/pan, lined

For the base

- 100 g/3½ oz/1 cup ground almonds
- 90 g/3¼ oz/scant ¾ cup chickpea (gram) flour
- 2½ tbsp maple syrup
- 2 tbsp coconut oil, melted
- 3 tbsp milk of choice
- a pinch of flaky sea salt

For the caramel

- 120 g/4 oz pitted Medjool dates
- 2 tbsp peanut butter
- 1 tbsp tahini
- 1 tbsp coconut oil, melted
- a pinch of flaky sea salt

For the chocolate

- 80 g/2¾ oz dark/bittersweet chocolate
- 1 tsp coconut oil

1. Preheat the oven to 160°C fan/180°C/350°F/gas mark 4.
2. To make the base, mix the ground almonds, chickpea flour, maple syrup, melted coconut oil, milk and salt in a bowl until it forms a thick sandy dough. Tip into the tin and press firmly and evenly into the base with your fingers.
3. Bake for 15 minutes, or until lightly golden. Remove from the oven and leave in the tin to cool completely.
4. Meanwhile, soak the dates in boiling water for 10 minutes. Drain, reserving 50 ml/1¾ fl oz/3½ tablespoons of the soaking liquid.
5. For the caramel, blend the soaked dates with the reserved liquid, peanut butter, tahini, melted coconut oil and a generous pinch of flaky salt, until smooth and thick.
6. Spread the caramel evenly over the base and smooth the surface. Freeze for at least 1 hour until the caramel is firm.
7. Melt the dark chocolate with the coconut oil in the microwave in 15-second intervals, then pour over the caramel. Use the back of a spoon to spread the chocolate into a thin, even layer. Return to the freezer for 10–15 minutes to allow the chocolate to harden.
8. Once completely set, lift from the tin and, using a warm knife for clean edges, slice into 12 bars (3 lines vertically, 4 lines horizontally).

Future you:

- Store in an airtight container in the fridge for up to 5 days.
- Cool and insert a piece of parchment paper between each bar. Stack and freeze for up to 1 month.
- Thaw in the fridge overnight.

Index

Note: page numbers in *bold* refer to illustrations.

T

V

W

Y

Z

Thank Yous

Despite my name being on the front cover, nothing about this gorgeous book you're holding in your hands is a one-person job. From the very beginning, so many people have poured their love, time and energy into bringing it to life, and I think we can all agree it's an absolute belter (biased, but correct!).

To my wonderful publishing team at Pavilion, thank you for once again believing in my vision and trusting me to build on the world of Healthy-ish. Ellen, my brilliant editor, thank you again for your guidance, friendship and for always knowing when to push me and when to reassure me. And Alice, thank you once again for steering the design with such care and creativity – we ended up with such a beautiful sister to book one. Laura, Caroline, Kom, Clare, Kate, and everyone else behind the scenes who has worked on this book in ways big and small, I'm endlessly grateful. Its success is as much yours as it is mine.

A huge thank you to Emily, my literary agent, for always going above and beyond to support me through the whole publication process. Thank you for your wisdom, honesty and constant encouragement. And to Ellie and Lucia, my brand agents and absolute dream team, thank you for having my back in every sense of the phrase. My job is far more fun and enjoyable with you both in it.

To the shoot team who made the entire photography process an absolute hoot. We laughed a lot, but we also worked so beautifully together, and I think that joy is woven through every image. Lucy, Holly, Eden and Louie, thank you for your talent, your energy and for bringing these recipes to life so effortlessly. The finished shots continue to take my breath away.

Now, to my wonderful family: Mum, Dad, Tom, Steph, Ottie and the entire Petersen/Bagot crew. I wish I had more words to say thank you for your constant love and for backing me through every twist and turn along the way. You've never once doubted me (even when you probably should have!), and that belief has meant everything.

To my gorgeous partner, Matt. Juggling Ironman training, writing this book and continuing to build my platforms got a lot at times, and I definitely wasn't always my most chilled self...! But you never stopped being my biggest supporter and my best friend. I am so grateful for you. And to Ilse, my soul sister, constant cheerleader and safe place. My life is so much better for having you in it.

To my online community, some of you have been here for over ten years (crazy!) and some of you are brand new, but every single one of you has played a part in making this happen. Thank you for growing with me over the years and for always showing up with kindness and enthusiasm. Your support means everything, and you are a huge part of why I get to do what I love.

And last but not least, YOU! I may have poured my heart and soul into these pages, but you're the one who chose to pick this book up, to cook from it, to dog-ear and dirty the pages and to welcome these recipes into your kitchen. That truly is a privilege I will never take for granted. Thank you.

With love,

Emma x

Pavilion
An imprint of HarperCollins*Publishers* Ltd
1 London Bridge Street
London SE1 9GF

www.harpercollins.co.uk

HarperCollins*Publishers*
Macken House
39/40 Mayor Street Upper
Dublin 1
D01 C9W8
Ireland

10 9 8 7 6 5 4 3 2 1

First published in Great Britain by Pavilion
An imprint of HarperCollins*Publishers* 2026

Emma Petersen asserts the moral right to be identified as the author of this work. A catalogue record of this book is available from the British Library.

ISBN 9780008772604

Publishing Director: Laura Russell
Commissioning Editor: Ellen Simmons
Editorial Assistants: Daisy Gudmunsen and Abigail Muth
Design Manager: Alice Kennedy-Owen
Production Controller: Grace O'Byrne
Photographer: Lucy Richards
Food Stylist: Holly Cowgill
Prop Stylist: Louie Waller
Cover/Layout Designer: Studio Nic + Lou
Copyeditor: Kate Reeves-Brown
Nutrionist: Clare Gray
Proofreader: Vicki Murrell
Indexer: Lisa Footit

Printed and bound by GPS Group in Bosnia and Herzegovina.

WHEN USING KITCHEN APPLIANCES PLEASE ALWAYS FOLLOW THE MANUFACTURER'S INSTRUCTIONS